A Wine & Food Affair

Tasting Along the Wine Road

COOKBOOK

A COLLECTION OF RECIPES FROM
"A Wine & Food Affair"

VOLUME 15

Recipes from the Wineries and Lodgings of the
Alexander, Dry Creek and Russian River Valleys.

WINE ROAD
NORTHERN SONOMA COUNTY

A custom cookbook published by

Wine Road Northern Sonoma County

P.O. Box 46, Healdsburg, CA 95448

wineroad.com

Content © Wine Road Northern Sonoma County

Design © Pembroke Studios, pembrokestudios.com

Illustrations © Chris Witkowski, chriswitkowski.com

Lodging and Winery photos © Lenny Siegel, siegelphotographic.com

Bottle shots © Kelly McManus, kellymcmanusphotography.com

Editor © Linda Murphy, anhonestdrink.com

ISBN 978 0 615 82636 3

Printed in China

TABLE OF CONTENTS

TABLE OF CONTENTS

TABLE OF CONTENTS

TABLE OF CONTENTS

FOREWORD

JESSE MALLGREN

EXECUTIVE CHEF, MADRONA MANOR, HEALDSBURG

A DAY IN THE LIFE OF A SONOMA CHEF

"George is a local fisherman who catches halibut the old-fashioned way, with a hook and line, in the waters surrounding the Golden Gate Bridge."

IT'S 6 A.M. AND MY CHILDREN ARE STILL asleep when my phone hums next to me. I jump out of bed and quickly tiptoe to my kitchen; I don't want to wake the kids. It's my fishmonger on the line; something is wrong.

"Jesse, the salmon boat did not come in."

"Anything local? How is the halibut?"

"It's beautiful. George just dropped off five fish this morning." George is a local fisherman who catches halibut the old-fashioned way, with a hook and line, in the waters surrounding the Golden Gate Bridge. I've cooked with George's fish for years, and they are always pristine and incredibly fresh.

"Perfect," I tell my fishmonger.

Wiley and Lilly, my son and daughter, are waking up and it's time for me to make coffee and breakfast. My coffee ritual is all about precision: 23 grams of coffee beans, freshly ground, 350 ml of water at 195° F. I use the "pour-over drip" method, which takes a full four minutes, but the coffee is smoothly textured and the flavors sing. Today the kids want fried eggs with buttered toast and peaches, so I collect the eggs from our backyard chickens, grab peaches from my neighbor and get to work. We sit down as a family and eat.

After the kids are off to school, I head to the farmers market for something to serve with the halibut dish I'll prepare for tonight's dinner service. I find some beautiful dry-farmed potatoes and a couple pounds of garlic scapes.

When I arrive at work, I head up the hill to start my daily walk through the garden. Madrona Manor sits on eight acres, one of which comprises our garden, where we source roughly 20% of our produce. Today, most of our tomatoes are not quite ripe, but that doesn't mean I can't use them. I pluck a few green tomatoes and put them in my basket. I find a few ripe cherry tomatoes and carefully place them in the basket as well. My plan is to roast the green tomatoes over charcoal, then steep them in a broth made from the halibut bones; I'll use this as a sauce for the fish. The cherry tomatoes will be peeled to show off their sweetness. I pick and taste a few more herbs and vegetables and choose the final ingredients to complete the dish.

Our local halibut is a lean fish, so to add a touch of richness, I poach the fish in extra virgin olive oil, heated to 130°, for 15 minutes. This process makes the fish tender yet flaky, and that will help it retain all of its natural juices. I roast the potatoes in salt to maintain the delicate earthy flavor of a dry-farmed potato. I then roast the garlic scapes (which have a very short season so I always make sure to grab them when they're available) with a type of seaweed called kombu, plus a splash of white soy sauce and a sprig of thyme.

The staff and I prepare the dish in its entirety and then taste it — something we do with every dish before we serve it to our guests. It is missing something, so I head back up the hill to our garden.

"Aha!" I spy borage, a plant with beautiful blue flowers and that tastes faintly of cucumbers. The borage will not only lighten up the halibut dish, it will look stunning on the plate. I rush back to the kitchen and make the addition. We taste the dish again, and know this time that it's perfect. Time for dinner service to begin!

"My plan is to roast the green tomatoes over charcoal, then steep them in a broth made from the halibut bones; I'll use this as a sauce for the fish. The cherry tomatoes will be peeled to show off their sweetness."

Photo Credit: Copyright 2012 Dylan +Jeni

RECIPES
from the wineries & lodgings

BRUNCH

Baked Eggs with Sautéed Mushrooms & Spinach

Lemon-Blueberry Buckle

Scrumptious Veggie Frittata

Strawberry-Banana French Toast

Chewy Airy Almond Cookies

Farmhouse Famous Scones

Sun-Dried Tomato Savory Biscuits

Perfect Brunch Pumpkin Bread

Bourbon-Fried Apples

Savory Ham, Artichoke & Cheese Strata

Tomato Basil Soup

Candied Applewood-Smoked Bacon

Dutch Baby with Apples & Honey

Humboldt Fog Cheese-Tomato Galette

Occidental Waffles with Brown Sugar Sauce

Wild King Salmon Carpaccio

Pumpkin Apple Cake

Raford's Healthy Harvest Granola

Ham & Cheese Bloated Breakfast Biscuits

Blueberry Pecan Scones

Bourbon Maple Cheesecake

The Blue Madame

Belle de Jour Inn

Bed & Breakfast

Tom and I first enjoyed this dish with a glass of Macon Villages wine in a quiet bistro in Paris. This led us to the purchase of individual copper gratin pans from E. Dehillerin, the most wonderful restaurant supply house, established in Paris in 1820. Our guests enjoy this brunch dish with mimosas.

16276 Healdsburg Avenue | Healdsburg, CA 95448
707-431-9777
belledejourinn.com

VEGI

BAKED EGGS
WITH SAUTÉED MUSHROOMS & SPINACH

SERVES 4

1 tablespoon olive oil

1 large leek, white and light green parts only, cut into ½-inch pieces

1 tablespoon unsalted butter

1 pound white or crimini mushrooms, thinly sliced (about 6 cups)

¼ cup dry white wine

5 ounces baby spinach

salt and freshly ground pepper

olive oil for coating ramekins

4 large eggs

small baguette, sliced diagonally and toasted

Preheat oven to 350°.

In a deep skillet, heat the olive oil. Add the leek and cook over moderate heat, stirring until the leek is softened, about 3 minutes. Stir in the butter and mushrooms. Cover and cook, stirring occasionally, until the mushrooms are softened and a lot of liquid is released, about 6 minutes.

Uncover the skillet and add the white wine, cooking over moderately high heat and stirring until the liquid is reduced to 2 tablespoons, about 5 minutes. Add the spinach and stir until the leaves are just wilted, about 2 minutes. Season with salt and pepper.

Coat 4 1-cup ramekins or small gratin dishes with olive oil. Transfer the mushroom-spinach mixture to the ramekins and crack an egg on top of each. Bake for 10-12 minutes, until the whites are set and yolks are still a bit runny. Remove the ramekins from the oven and let the eggs stand for 2 minutes; serve with toast.

CALDERWOOD
INN

I like to combine the dry ingredients the night before and finish mixing and baking the cake when I arrive at the inn in the morning. Once the cake goes into the oven, the wonderful smell permeates the inn, and guests are eager to arrive at my table on time!

25 W. Grant Street | Healdsburg, CA 95448
707-431-1110
calderwoodinn.com

VEGI

LEMON-BLUEBERRY
BUCKLE

SERVES 8-10

STREUSEL TOPPING

6 tablespoons flour

6 tablespoons sugar

¼ teaspoon salt

4 tablespoons cold
   unsalted butter

CAKE

1-¾ cups flour

1 teaspoon baking powder

½ teaspoon baking soda

½ teaspoon salt

¾ cup unsalted butter,
   room temperature

1 cup sugar

2 large eggs

1 teaspoon vanilla

2 tablespoons lemon juice

zest of ½ lemon

¾ cup whole-milk yogurt

8 ounces fresh blueberries
   (blackberries and cranberries
   also work well)

Preheat oven to 350°.

To prepare the streusel, mix together the flour, sugar and salt in a small bowl. Make a crumble by mixing the butter into the dry ingredients with your hands. Refrigerate the streusel while you make the cake.

To prepare the cake, sift the flour, baking powder, baking soda and salt together in a large bowl and set it aside.

In another bowl, beat the butter, sugar and eggs together with an electric mixer, until the mixture is light and fluffy, about 2 minutes. Add the vanilla, lemon juice, zest and yogurt and beat on low speed until the ingredients come together; the batter should have some lumps in it. Then add the dry ingredients and stir until just combined; do not overmix. Gently fold in the blueberries.

Spread the batter into a 9-inch cake pan that has been coated with nonstick spray. Sprinkle the streusel evenly over the top of the cake. Bake until the top is golden brown and the center no longer jiggles, about 55 minutes.

Cool for at least 15 minutes before cutting the buckle into wedges and serving.

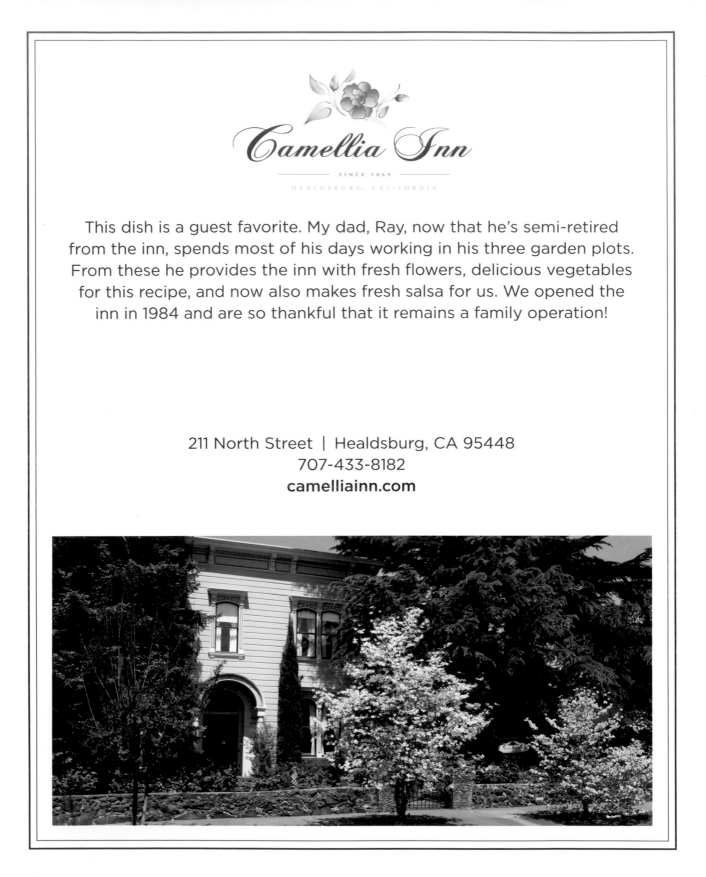

Camellia Inn

SINCE 1869
HEALDSBURG, CALIFORNIA

This dish is a guest favorite. My dad, Ray, now that he's semi-retired from the inn, spends most of his days working in his three garden plots. From these he provides the inn with fresh flowers, delicious vegetables for this recipe, and now also makes fresh salsa for us. We opened the inn in 1984 and are so thankful that it remains a family operation!

211 North Street | Healdsburg, CA 95448
707-433-8182
camelliainn.com

SCRUMPTIOUS
VEGGIE FRITTATA

SERVES 12

2-3 fresh zucchini squash

2 cups Parmesan cheese, grated or shredded

1 cup mushrooms

2 large tomatoes

14 eggs

2 cups mayonnaise

8-10 basil leaves

¼ cup green onions, chopped

Preheat oven to 350°.

Grease a 9-inch by 15-inch casserole dish.

Cut the zucchinis crossways into ¼-inch slices. Layer ½ of the zucchini slices in the bottom of the pan and sprinkle them with ½ of the Parmesan.

Dice the mushrooms and layer ½ of them on top of the cheese. Over the mushrooms, layer the remaining zucchini, the remaining mushrooms, and the remaining Parmesan. Cut the tomatoes into ½-inch slices and layer them on top of the cheese.

In a large bowl, lightly beat the eggs and then add the mayonnaise. Chop the basil leaves and add them to the mixture. Beat well.

Pour the egg mixture on top of the vegetables and bake for 45 minutes to 1 hour, or until the center of the casserole is firm.

You can assemble the vegetables and cheese in the dish and prepare the egg mixture the night before. Refrigerate them overnight. The next morning, pour the egg mixture over the vegetables and bake as directed above. Let cool and serve.

English Tea Garden Inn

I first made this recipe when we lived in Pennsylvania. We had gone on a ski trip with friends and we each took turns making breakfast. This dish was the big hit of the weekend and all our guests at the inn love it, too. It's especially good on a cold winter's day.

119 West Third Street | Cloverdale, CA 95425
800-996-8675
teagardeninn.com

STRAWBERRY-BANANA
FRENCH TOAST

SERVES 8

1 loaf French bread

5 eggs

¾ cup milk

¼ teaspoon baking powder

1 tablespoon vanilla extract

1 16-ounce bag frozen
   strawberries

4 ripe bananas, sliced

1 cup sugar

1 tablespoon apple pie spice

cinnamon sugar blend

Start this recipe the night before you plan to serve it.

Cut the bread into 8 thick slices and place them in a single layer in a deep-sided dish.

In a medium bowl, combine the eggs, milk, baking powder and vanilla extract. Pour the mixture over the bread slices; cover and refrigerate the dish overnight.

The next morning, preheat the oven to 450°.

Combine the strawberries, bananas, sugar and apple pie spice in a large bowl. Spread the fruit mixture in a greased 9-inch by 13-inch baking dish and top with the prepared bread slices. Sprinkle with cinnamon sugar and bake for 25 minutes.

To serve, place 1 slice of bread on each plate and spoon the fruit sauce from the baking dish over the top.

February 10, 2013, was Chinese New Year, the year of the Snake. As always, on New Year's Eve our family and extended family get together for a dinner that features some traditional dishes only served during the New Year. For one of our desserts, I decided to do a riff on the normal almond cookie you might find in Chinatown. The cookie turned out to be very easy to make and would be a great light ending to a Sunday brunch.

101 Gravenstein Highway South | Sebastopol, CA 95472
707-829-6677
winecountryhi.com

VEGI

CHEWY AIRY
ALMOND COOKIES

MAKES 20 COOKIES

3 egg whites

1-½ cups sugar

2-¾ cups ground almonds or almond flour

20 whole almonds, for garnish

Preheat oven to 350°.

Crack the eggs and separate the yolks from the whites. Pour the whites into a bowl and with a hand mixer or freestanding mixer, beat the whites into soft peaks. Add the sugar and beat until the whites are stiff and a glossy-white color.

Add the ground almonds or almond flour, and using a rubber spatula, fold carefully into the whites, until the mixture is evenly combined. If the mixture is too thin, add more almonds/almond flour to thicken it. Both the thin and thicker dough produces very light, slightly chewy cookies, although the thicker dough doesn't spread as much while the cookies bake.

Line a cookie sheet with parchment paper and scoop 1-tablespoon balls of dough onto the sheet, spacing them well apart. Place a whole almond on the top of each cookie and bake until golden, about 14 minutes.

FARMHOUSE

This is our master recipe for scones, and we add seasonal ingredients to dress them up. In the fall, we incorporate dried figs, fresh apples, fresh pears, fresh or candied ginger, or cinnamon glaze. In winter, citrus zest, candied citrus rind, dried currants, cranberries and raisins are added to the dough before baking. Spring calls for fresh strawberries, blueberries and raspberries, and summer scones feature peaches, nectarines, plums and pitted cherries. Year-round, we use toasted nuts, coconut, and white or chocolate chips.

7871 River Road | Forestville, CA 95436
707-887-3300
farmhouseinn.com

FARMHOUSE

FAMOUS SCONES

MAKES 12 SCONES

2-¼ cups flour

⅓ cup sugar

1 tablespoon baking powder

1-½ sticks chilled unsalted
   butter, cut into cubes

¾ cup heavy cream

sanding sugar, for dusting

Preheat oven to 400°.

Combine all the dry ingredients with an electric mixer or food processor. Pulse until the mixture is just combined.

Add in the butter cubes, mixing or pulsing on low until the mixture resembles a fine-ground meal. Add the cream in the same method.

Turn the dough onto parchment paper or a lightly floured surface. Gently form the dough into a round disk approximately 1-½ inches thick. Cut the disk in ½ and then cut wedges from each ½ to the size of scone desired.

Brush each scone with cream, dust with sanding sugar, and bake on a parchment-lined baking sheet placed in the center of the oven, for 12-16 minutes, until the bottoms of the scones are golden brown. Alternatively, glaze the scones after baking with powdered sugar mixed with cream, citrus or spices.

We serve these biscuits every day, and they're a great accompaniment to sliced ham. Try adding other savory ingredients when making these biscuits, including bacon pieces, garlic and rosemary. Or replace the mustard powder, tomatoes and cheese with vanilla, cinnamon or lavender for a sweeter biscuit. The yummy possibilities are endless!

16650 River Road (Highway 116) | Guerneville, CA 95446
888-243-2674
ferngrove.com

SUN-DRIED TOMATO
SAVORY BISCUITS

MAKES 15 BISCUITS

2-½ cups self-rising flour

1 teaspoon sugar

1 teaspoon mustard powder

½ cup unsalted butter, chilled
   and cut into cubes

small handful sun-dried
   (not oil-packed) tomatoes,
   chopped into ½-inch pieces

1 cup buttermilk

melted butter, for brushing

1 cup sharp Cheddar cheese,
   shredded

Preheat oven to 425°.

Place the flour, sugar and mustard powder in a medium bowl. Add the cubes of cold butter and cut them into the mixture with a pastry blender or by hand. Stir in the sun-dried tomatoes, then the buttermilk, until the mixture holds together.

On a floured surface, knead the dough lightly about 6 times. Pat or roll it to approximately ½-inch thickness. Cut the dough into rounds with a 2-inch cutter. Place the rounds on an ungreased baking sheet and bake for 5 minutes. Turn the tray and bake for an additional 5-6 minutes.

Remove the biscuits from the oven and brush their tops with melted butter. Sprinkle the cheese on top and serve warm.

Hint: For soft sides, place the biscuits on the baking pan with their sides touching. When cutting out the biscuits, don't twist the cutter. This lets the sides of the biscuits to rise in fluffy layers.

Feel the Hamptonality™

Baking and gifting treats has long been my way of showing love, support and appreciation. Luckily, my baking skills have become more refined since I was 7 and baked what must have been the worst batch of cookies ever. I developed this bread recipe after being challenged to make a pumpkin bread that rivaled that made by a co-worker's mom. I tried different versions and came up one ideal for brunch.

8937 Brooks Road South | Windsor, CA 95492
707-837-9355
windsorcasuites.hamptoninn.com

VEGI

PERFECT BRUNCH
PUMPKIN BREAD

MAKES 3 STANDARD/ 9 MINI LOAVES

1 15-ounce can pumpkin (not pumpkin pie filling)

4 eggs

1 cup vegetable oil

2/3 cup water

2-½ cups sugar

¼ cup brown sugar

3-½ cups all-purpose flour

2 teaspoons baking soda

½ teaspoon baking powder

1-½ teaspoons salt

1-½ teaspoons ground cinnamon

1 teaspoon ground nutmeg

½ teaspoon ground ginger

OPTIONAL ADD-INS:

½ cup mini semisweet chocolate chips

½ cup walnuts or pecans

½ cup dried fruit

Preheat oven to 350°.

Spray loaf pans with nonstick spray.

In a large bowl or stand mixer, mix together the first 6 ingredients until they're smooth.

In a separate large bowl, mix together the remaining (dry) ingredients.

Slowly incorporate the dry ingredients into the wet; mix just until the batter comes together. Pour the batter evenly into loaf pans and bake for approximately 45 minutes for a standard pan, 25 minutes for mini loaf pans. The bread is done when a toothpick inserted into the thickest portion comes out clean.

Let the bread rest for 10 minutes before taking it out of the pan; let it rest another 5 minutes before slicing it.

The Haydon Street Inn
Bed & Breakfast

John Harasty, owner of the Haydon Street Inn, was the former executive chef at Churchill Downs racetrack in Louisville, Ky. He developed this breakfast recipe, finishing the apples with bourbon, as a way to pay homage to the time he lived in Kentucky.

321 Haydon Street | Healdsburg, CA 95448
707-433-5228
haydon.com

VEGI

BOURBON-FRIED
APPLES

SERVES 4

canola oil for frying

1 large flour tortilla, cut in
⅛-inch-wide strips

2 tablespoons cinnamon sugar
blend (for tortilla strips)

5 Fuji apples, peeled, cored
and sliced

1 tablespoon butter

1 tablespoon cinnamon sugar
blend (for apples)

2 ounces bourbon

Heat the canola oil in a deep fryer to 350°. Add the tortilla strips and fry them until they are lightly browned. Remove the strips from the fryer and let them cool in a bowl lined with paper towels, to absorb the extra oil. Toss the strips with cinnamon sugar and set aside to cool.

While the tortilla strips cool, peel, core and slice the apples.

Melt the butter in a skillet and add the apples. Sauté the apples until they are no longer crunchy, then sprinkle with 1 tablespoon of cinnamon sugar. Add the bourbon. Let the bourbon cook down for about 2 minutes before serving with the crispy tortilla strips.

GUERNEVILLE
RUSSIAN RIVER

I love recipes that make me appear to be brilliant and inspired. Better yet, I like ones that allow me to prep ahead and then pop the dish in the oven when guests arrive. Stratas are perfect for this. By the time I go to bed, breakfast is all but done. I adapted this recipe from an old issue of Bon Appetit magazine. It looks heavy on the herbs, but it all works really well together and doesn't come out too strongly flavored, just very distinctive. Freeze leftover portions in a zip-close bag.

14000 Woodland Drive | Guerneville, CA 95446
707-869-0333
highlandsresort.com

SAVORY HAM, ARTICHOKE & CHEESE
STRATA

SERVES 8-10

8 large eggs

4 cups whole milk or half and half

1 tablespoon garlic, chopped

1-½ teaspoons salt

¾ teaspoon black pepper

½ teaspoon ground nutmeg

2 tablespoons fresh sage, chopped

1 tablespoon fresh thyme, chopped

1-½ teaspoons herbes de Provence

8 cups sourdough bread, cut into 1-inch cubes

12 ounces smoked ham, chopped

3 jars (6-½ ounces) marinated artichoke hearts, drained and roughly chopped (remove any leaves that look too fibrous)

8 ounces fresh goat cheese, softened and crumbled

2-½ cups (packed) grated fontina cheese

Start this recipe the night before you plan to serve it.

Beat the eggs well and stir in the milk or half and half. In a small bowl, mix together the garlic, salt, pepper, nutmeg, sage, thyme and herbes de Provence. Coat a 9-inch by 13-inch glass baking dish with nonstick spray.

Place a layer of bread in the dish, followed by a generous sprinkling of the herb mixture. Add 1 layer each of ham, artichokes, goat cheese and fontina, top with another layer of bread, and repeat the layering in the above order, finishing with the remaining fontina.

Pour the egg/milk mixture over the top of the strata and cover the dish tightly with clinging plastic wrap. Squish the bread down as you pull the plastic wrap tight, so that all the bread is submerged in the liquid. Refrigerate for at least 8 hours.

The next morning, preheat the oven to 350°.

Place the chilled strata on a rimmed cookie sheet and let it come to room temperature for 15 minutes. Remove the plastic wrap and bake the strata for 45 minutes to 1 hour. It's done when the cheese puffs up and turns golden brown; the filling should be firm. Slice with a sharp knife and serve.

TOMATO BASIL SOUP

SERVES 12

10 Roma tomatoes

extra virgin olive oil

salt and pepper

1-½ tablespoons garlic, minced

1 cup yellow onion, diced

1 bunch sweet basil

½ bunch parsley

2 teaspoons fresh thyme, chopped

7 cups canned diced tomatoes

¾ cup heavy cream

¾ cup chicken stock

Preheat oven to 350°.

Cut the Roma tomatoes in ½ and place them on a baking sheet. Drizzle the tomatoes with olive oil and sprinkle them with salt and pepper. Bake until they wilt and begin to blacken at the edges. Set aside.

In a large saucepan, sauté the garlic and onion until they're fragrant. Add the basil, parsley and thyme and sauté until well incorporated. Add the canned tomatoes and simmer for 1 hour.

Place the contents of the saucepan in a blender, along with the roasted Roma tomatoes, and blend into a smooth texture. Pour the blender contents back into the saucepan, then add the heavy cream and chicken stock. Heat until 165° and serve.

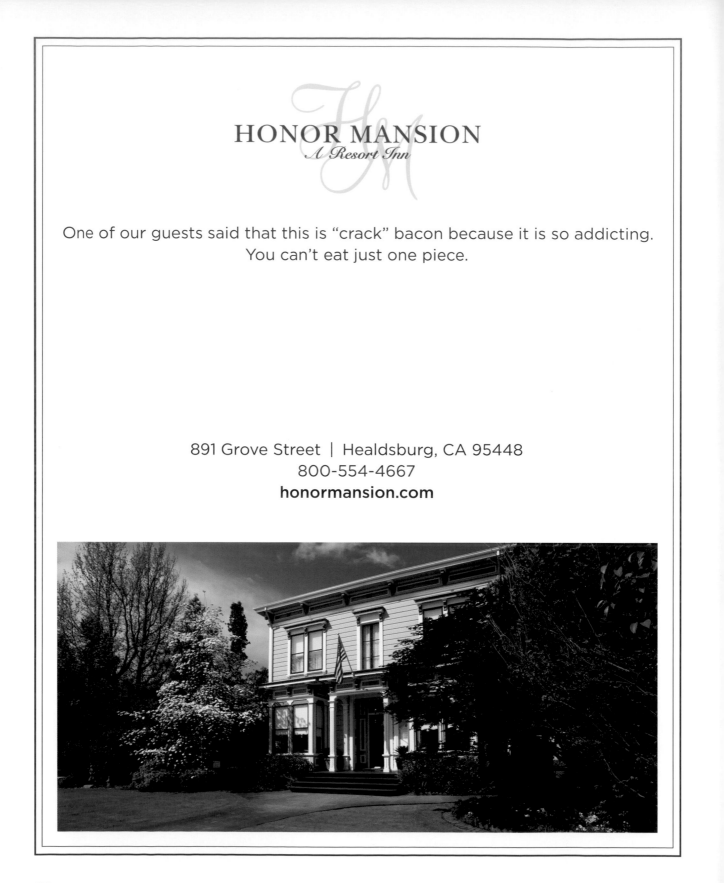

HONOR MANSION
A Resort Inn

One of our guests said that this is "crack" bacon because it is so addicting. You can't eat just one piece.

891 Grove Street | Healdsburg, CA 95448
800-554-4667
honormansion.com

CANDIED APPLEWOOD-SMOKED
BACON
(AKA "CRACK BACON")

MAKES 10-15 SLICES

1 cup maple syrup

1 tablespoon Dijon mustard

1 pound applewood-smoked
   bacon

black pepper, ground

Preheat oven to 350°.

In a small bowl, mix the maple syrup and mustard.

Place the bacon slices on a cooling rack and brush the top side of each one with the syrup-mustard glaze. Bake the bacon on the rack for 20 minutes.

Turn the slices over, glaze the other side, and bake for another 20 minutes. The bacon needs to be thoroughly cooked, to a dark color, or it will look greasy. Remove the bacon from the oven and sprinkle with finely ground black pepper and serve.

Hope-Merrill House

A Dutch Baby is a cross between a pancake and a popover that is cooked in a cast-iron skillet. Often called a German pancake, it's light and airy, with a tender, puffed-up center and crispy edges. Serve it at the table, right from the skillet.

21253 Geyserville Avenue | Geyserville, CA 95441
800-825-4233
hope-inns.com

VEGI

DUTCH BABY
WITH APPLES & HONEY

SERVES 4

4 tablespoons unsalted butter

4 large eggs

1 cup milk

1 cup flour

¼ teaspoon salt

¼ teaspoon vanilla

2 tart apples

2 tablespoons butter, for apples

½ cup honey

3 teaspoons lemon juice

½ teaspoon cardamom

1 teaspoon cinnamon

Preheat oven to 425°.

Cut the butter into small pieces and place them in a cast-iron skillet without the lid on. Place the skillet in the hot oven to melt the butter.

Place the eggs in a blender and blend until they're foamy. Add the milk, flour, salt and vanilla and blend until the batter is combined.

When the butter has fully melted in the oven, carefully remove the skillet and swirl the butter to coat the pan. Quickly pour the batter into the skillet and return it to the hot oven. Bake for 25 minutes, or until the Dutch Baby is puffed and lightly browned.

Quarter and core the apples, removing the seeds. Cut the apples into thin slices. Melt 2 tablespoons of butter in a sauté pan. Add the apples, honey, lemon juice, cardamom and cinnamon and cook until the apples are just tender.

Pour the apple mixture onto the cooked Dutch Baby, cut it into wedges, and serve hot.

HYATT®
VINEYARD CREEK
HOTEL & SPA
SONOMA COUNTY

I've known Mary Keehn of Cypress Grove Chevre for many years and her Humboldt Fog is my favorite cheese. At the restaurant, we make our own sun-dried tomatoes and I thought that they would be a perfect match for Humboldt Fog. I also love buttery puff pastry and I decided to wrap the cheese and tomatoes in it. The pastry is flaky, the cheese melty, and the tomatoes and glazed balsamic onions complement the cheese beautifully. Our goat cheese galette won the "Best Use of Cheese" award at the Sonoma County Fair four years in a row.

170 Railroad Street | Santa Rosa, CA 95401
707-284-1234
vineyardcreek.hyatt.com

HUMBOLDT FOG CHEESE-TOMATO
GALETTE

SERVES 6

6 5-inch-square puff pastry
sheets

6 tablespoons balsamic
red onions

12 sun-dried tomatoes

6 ounces Humboldt Fog goat
cheese, cut into 1-ounce
pieces

Prepare your favorite recipe for balsamic-glazed red onions.

Preheat oven to 450°.

Lay out the 6 sheets of puff pastry on a clean, lightly floured work surface. Spoon 1 tablespoon of balsamic red onions into the center of each sheet and top the onions with 2 sun-dried tomatoes. Place a 1-ounce piece of Humboldt Fog cheese on top of the tomatoes.

Fold the puff pastry sides over the filling and twist the corners at the top to form a pinwheel. Bake the galette until it's golden brown, about 8-10 minutes.

Serve the galette with a small mixed-green salad.

Inn at OCCIDENTAL

This recipe was created entirely by accident. We made waffles with sour cream and have always received rave reviews. One sleepy morning, we grabbed the yogurt instead of the sour cream container. After the yogurt was added, we realized our mistake but it was too late ... breakfast was minutes from being served. But the waffle that resulted was even better than our original version. The yogurt created a crisper waffle and we figured it saved a few calories. Thus, our accidental Occidental waffles were born and we have been serving them ever since.

3657 Church Street | Occidental, CA 95465
707-874-1047
innatoccidental.com

OCCIDENTAL

WAFFLES

WITH BROWN SUGAR SAUCE

SERVES 8

BROWN SUGAR SAUCE

1 cup brown sugar

½ cup water

2 tablespoons light corn syrup

½ cup heavy cream

1 teaspoon vanilla extract

WAFFLES

2 cups white flour

2-½ teaspoons baking powder

¼ teaspoon baking soda

½ teaspoon salt

4-½ teaspoons sugar

4 eggs, separated

1 cup plain yogurt

1-½ cups whole milk

1 cup less 2 tablespoons
   melted butter

pinch cream of tartar

1 teaspoon vanilla extract

To prepare the brown sugar sauce, combine the sugar, water and corn syrup in a saucepan. Bring the mixture to a simmer and cook, stirring occasionally, for 5 minutes. Stir in the heavy cream and continue to simmer until the sauce thickens slightly, about 5 minutes. Stir in the vanilla and keep the sauce warm.

To make the waffles, sift together the first 5 (dry) ingredients. In a separate bowl, beat the egg yolks, yogurt, milk and melted butter. Add the liquid ingredients to the dry and mix together thoroughly.

Add the cream of tartar to the egg whites and beat them with a mixer on high speed, until they form stiff peaks. Fold ⅓ of the egg white mixture into the batter. When incorporated, add the remaining egg whites and fold them in completely. Stir in the vanilla.

Bake on a waffle iron, and serve with the warm brown sugar sauce.

Note: For a richer waffle, substitute the yogurt with sour cream.

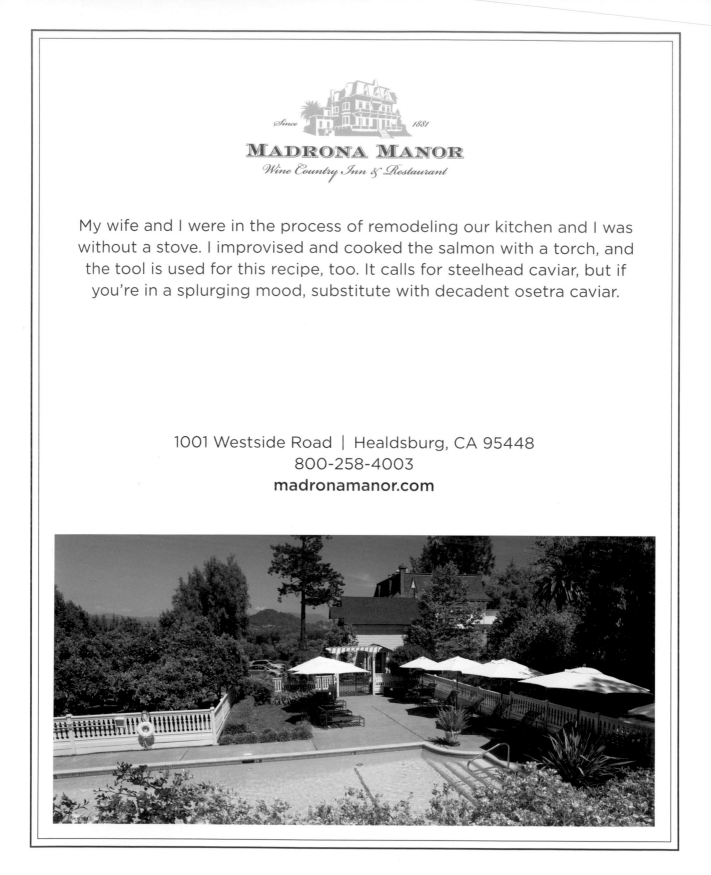

MADRONA MANOR
Wine Country Inn & Restaurant
Since 1881

My wife and I were in the process of remodeling our kitchen and I was without a stove. I improvised and cooked the salmon with a torch, and the tool is used for this recipe, too. It calls for steelhead caviar, but if you're in a splurging mood, substitute with decadent osetra caviar.

1001 Westside Road | Healdsburg, CA 95448
800-258-4003
madronamanor.com

WILD KING SALMON

CARPACCIO

SERVES 4

8 ounces freshly caught king salmon filet, skin and pin bones removed

2 tablespoons extra virgin olive oil

1 tablespoon diced shallots

4 pinches kosher salt

1 lemon, halved

2 tablespoons smoked or standard crème fraiche

2 ounces steelhead caviar, preferably smoked

12 small sprigs watercress

4 slices brioche, toasted

Cut the salmon into 4 equal portions. Cover a cutting board with a large piece of plastic wrap and rub it with 1 teaspoon of the olive oil.

Place a piece of salmon in the center of the plastic wrap and cover it with a second piece of plastic. Using the bottom of a skillet, gently pound the salmon into a paper-thin sheet. Repeat the process for the other 3 pieces.

Remove the top sheet of plastic wrap on all 4 portions of pounded salmon and sprinkle the pieces evenly with the shallots. Sprinkle a pinch of salt over each fish piece, then gently transfer them to a well-chilled plate. Make sure the side of the salmon with the shallots and salt are on the bottom touching the plate.

Using a blow torch, gently cook the salmon with a back and forth motion of the flame. This should take about 8 seconds (you are cooking the salmon only halfway).

Squeeze lemon over the cooked salmon. Spoon a dollop of crème fraiche onto the center of each salmon piece and top with caviar. Place the watercress sprigs around the outside of the caviar and serve with freshly toasted brioche.

OLD CROCKER INN

Late afternoon or early evening, I always provide something freshly baked for guests to nibble on or come back for after dinner. This cake is especially good warm from the oven, but I leave it out overnight in the dining room on a covered cake stand, and it somehow disappears before breakfast the next day. It's easy to make and light enough to serve year-round.

1126 Old Crocker Inn Road | Cloverdale, CA 95425
707-894-4000
oldcrockerinn.com

PUMPKIN APPLE CAKE

SERVES UP TO 16

½ cup unsalted butter

1-½ cups sugar

2 eggs

1 teaspoon vanilla

2 medium red apples (Honeycrisp, Jonathan, Stayman), unpeeled and diced small

1 cup canned plain pumpkin

2 teaspoons orange zest

2 cups all-purpose flour

1 teaspoon baking powder

¾ teaspoon baking soda

½ teaspoon salt

½ teaspoon cinnamon

¼ teaspoon nutmeg

¼ teaspoon ground cloves

¼ teaspoon ground ginger

powdered sugar

Preheat oven to 350°.

Grease and flour a 9- or 10-inch Bundt pan.

In a bowl, cream the butter and beat in the sugar. Beat in the eggs 1 at a time. Stir in the vanilla, apples, pumpkin and orange zest.

Whisk the dry ingredients together and stir them into the pumpkin mixture just until blended. Spoon the batter into the Bundt pan and press it down to eliminate air pockets.

Bake the cake for 30 minutes and give the pan a ½ turn. Bake for another 15 minutes and check for doneness, when a toothpick inserted in the middle of the cake comes out clean.

Allow the cake to cool in the pan on a wire rack for 15 minutes. Turn it out onto the rack to continue to cool for another 20 minutes. Sprinkle powdered sugar on top of the cake and decorate with fresh flowers.

The Raford Inn
Bed and Breakfast

This is a recipe I made long before I bought the inn. We like to serve it as a starter, topped with organic vanilla yogurt and fresh berries. However, it is healthy and hearty enough as a stand-alone breakfast. Our guests love it and often ask for the recipe.

10630 Wohler Road | Healdsburg, CA 95448
707-887-9573
rafordinn.com

RAFORD'S HEALTHY HARVEST

GRANOLA

MAKES 6 CUPS

3 cups old-fashioned rolled oats

½ cup shredded coconut

½ cup sunflower seeds

⅔ cup sliced almonds

2 tablespoons raw sesame seeds

½ cup hulled green pumpkin seeds

2 tablespoons oat bran

2 tablespoons wheat germ

¼ cup butter

¼ cup honey

1 cup mixed dried berries

½ cup dried bananas

Preheat oven to 325°.

In a large bowl, stir together the rolled oats, coconut, sunflower seeds, almonds, sesame seeds, pumpkin seeds, oat bran and wheat germ.

In a small saucepan, melt the butter and honey over low heat, stirring constantly. Pour the butter mixture over the oat mixture and stir until the ingredients are well combined.

In a large jelly roll pan coated with nonstick spray, spread the granola evenly and bake it on the middle rack of the oven. Stir halfway through baking, and cook to golden brown, about 15 minutes total. Allow the granola to cool in the pan on a rack and stir in the dried fruits.

Granola can be stored in the freezer or kept in an airtight container at cool room temperature for about 2 weeks.

My dad was in the restaurant business when I was growing up in Oklahoma and I watched him experiment with all types of menu items. One of his experiments started with a variation on biscuits and gravy, where he stuffed a biscuit with sausage gravy and added more gravy on top. The variation I liked for breakfast is this ham and cheese biscuit. Once you see how easy it is, I guarantee that you, too, will want to come up with your own variations. It freezes beautifully!

20292 Highway 116 | Monte Rio, CA 95462
707-865-1143
riovilla.com

HAM & CHEESE BLOATED BREAKFAST

BISCUITS

MAKES 12 BISCUITS

FILLING

1 egg

2 tablespoons milk

½ cup diced cooked ham

¼ chopped onion

¼ cup shredded Cheddar cheese

½ teaspoon ground pepper

pinch of salt

BISCUITS

2 cups flour

1 tablespoon baking powder

¼ teaspoon baking soda

1 teaspoon salt

6 tablespoons butter, very cold

1 cup milk

Prepare the filling by beating the egg and milk into a smooth consistency. Stir in the remaining filling ingredients and set aside.

To prepare the biscuits, preheat the oven to 450° and generously coat a muffin tin with nonstick spray.

Combine the dry ingredients in a bowl, or pulse them in a food processor. Cut the butter into chunks and cut them into the flour mixture, until it resembles coarse meal. One trick is to cut up the butter beforehand and keep it in the freezer until needed. Add the milk to the course mixture and mix until just combined

Transfer the dough to a floured surface. Fold it 5 or 6 times, keeping it floured just enough to not stick. Press the dough into a 12-inch by 9-inch rectangle with your fingers; it should be about ¼-inch thick. Cut the dough into 3-inch squares and drape each in the muffin tin. Don't press them down completely, nor worry about covering the entire muffin cup.

Spoon the filling into the middle of each square. Start lightly and go back with more if necessary. Pull the 4 points of each square to the middle but do not completely enclose the filling, as the biscuits will rise and fill out during cooking. Bake for 12-14 minutes. Serve hot and garnish with more shredded cheese.

Sonoma Orchid Inn

These scones are perfect for make-ahead ease and fresh-baked goodness. Once the dough is prepared, you can form it into individual balls and freeze them for baking later.
Once frozen, place the scones in freezer storage bags.

12850 River Road | Guerneville, CA 95446
888-877-4466
sonomaorchidinn.com

VEGI

BLUEBERRY PECAN
SCONES

MAKES 12 SCONES

7 ounces cold unsalted butter

2-½ cups all-purpose flour

⅓ cup granulated sugar

1 teaspoon baking powder

½ teaspoon salt

¼ teaspoon baking soda

⅓ cup toasted pecans, chopped

1 cup buttermilk

½ cup fresh or frozen
   blueberries

Preheat oven to 375°.

Line 2 baking sheets with parchment paper. Chop the butter into ¼-inch pieces and spread them on a plate. Place the plate in the freezer until the butter pieces are hard, about 30 minutes or overnight. (It is important to make the pieces no larger than ¼-inch because they are difficult to make any smaller once frozen.)

In a large bowl, combine the flour, sugar, baking powder, salt and baking soda. Add the frozen butter, and chop the mixture with 2 butter knives or a pastry blender until it is well-blended and some of the butter is crumbly. Mix in the pecans. Gradually add the buttermilk, ⅓ cup at a time, and mix gently until all the ingredients are incorporated but not completely blended. You might not use up all of the liquid. The end result should be a shaggy mass.

Sprinkle the blueberries on top of the dough and mix only enough to evenly distribute them.

Gently form the dough into ⅓-cup balls and place them 1 inch apart on the prepared baking sheets. Bake for 24-26 minutes or until the scones are cooked through and golden. Let them cool 10 minutes before serving.

Village Inn & Restaurant

HOTEL • BAR • RESTAURANT ON THE RUSSIAN RIVER

What better way to end a brunch than with something decadent and special? This recipe is one that I have held onto like gold and has become a favorite among guests at the inn, as well as winning consecutive silver medals at the Sonoma County Harvest Fair. I hope you enjoy making and sharing this cheesecake as much as I do.

20822 River Boulevard | Monte Rio, CA 95462
707-865-2304
villageinn-ca.com

VEGI

BOURBON MAPLE
CHEESECAKE

SERVES 12

CRUST

1-½ cups graham cracker
crumbs

¾ cup sugar

½ cup unsalted butter, melted

1 tablespoon unsalted butter
(for greasing pan)

FILLING

3 pounds Philadelphia cream
cheese, room temperature

1 cup sugar

2 tablespoons heavy cream

1 tablespoon vanilla extract

3 eggs, lightly beaten

2 tablespoons cornstarch

4 ounces Jim Beam bourbon

¾ cup maple syrup

To prepare the crust, mix the graham cracker crumbs and sugar thoroughly, then add the melted butter. Grease a 10-inch springform pan with butter and press the mixture firmly into the pan. Chill the crust in the refrigerator for approximately 45 minutes (but not overnight).

Preheat oven to 325°.

To prepare the filling, cut the cream cheese into small chunks and place them in a large bowl. Add the sugar and stir until the mixture is creamy. Add the heavy cream and vanilla and mix well. Add the lightly beaten eggs to the bowl and blend until smooth. Sift in the cornstarch and mix again. Add the bourbon and maple syrup and blend the filling until it's smooth.

Pour the filling into the chilled crust and bake for 1-½ hours or until the center doesn't wiggle when the pan is tapped firmly. Remove the cheesecake from the oven, allow it to cool on a rack for at least 1 hour, then chill it in the refrigerator for 5 hours or more before serving.

VINTNERS INN

At Vintners Inn, we have a signature blueberry jam infused with orange liqueur and vanilla bean. Thinking of a distinctive way we could utilize it, I added it to a classic French dish that is perfect for brunch, the Croque Madame. With toasted sourdough, ham and Gruyere topped with a Mornay sauce and broiled – I thought the sweetness and round flavor of the jam would offset the salty ham and cut the richness of the cheese sauce. Thus, the Blue Madame. Top it with a sunny-side-up egg, and it's a great way to start a day in Sonoma County.

4330 Barnes Road | Santa Rosa, CA 95403
707-575-7350
vintnersinn.com

THE BLUE MADAME

SERVES 4

2-½ tablespoons butter

3 tablespoons all-purpose flour

2 cups milk

salt and pepper, to taste

pinch nutmeg

4 ounces Gruyere cheese, grated

8 slices sourdough bread, toasted

¼ cup of your favorite blueberry jam

4 thick slices ham

4 slices Gruyere cheese

4 tablespoons butter

4 eggs

To prepare the sauce, heat the butter in a small saucepan. Whisk in the flour and cook until the mixture comes together, about 1 minute. Slowly whisk in the milk. Bring the mixture to a boil, reduce the heat and simmer for 2 minutes. Add the salt, pepper and nutmeg. Remove the pan from the heat and whisk in the grated Gruyere until it's melted.

Preheat the broiler.

On a ½ sheet pan, place 4 pieces of toast and spread the top of each with 2 tablespoons of blueberry jam. Top each with 1 slice of ham, followed by 1 slice of Gruyere. Place the toasts under the broiler until the cheese is melted, about 1-2 minutes. Place the remaining 4 slices of toast on each sandwich. Spoon a generous amount of mornay sauce over each and broil until the sauce is bubbling and browned, about 3 minutes.

Heat the butter in a nonstick skillet, add the eggs and cook them sunny side up, until the whites are set and yolks still runny. Season with salt and pepper, and top each sandwich with an egg. Then enjoy!

APPETIZERS

Curried Chicken Tartlets

Golden Beet Croquettes with Meyer Lemon Salt

Parrilla-Grilled New York Steak with Romesco & Braised Mushrooms

Smoked Duroc Pork Tenderloin with Porcini Flan

Prosciutto 'Maki Roll'

Classic Italian Fonduta con Tartufi

Grilled Rosemary Steak Skewers with Parmesan Sauce

Slow-Roasted Italian Pulled Pork with Zinfandel Sauce

Dakine Kahlua Pork Sliders

Truffled Croque Madame with Quail Egg

Lamb Crostini with Chermoula Aioli

King Salmon Cakes

Shrimp on a Stick with Inflated Wild Rice

Ahh-Hee Tuna & Avocado Salad on Endive

Poisson Cru Ahi Cones with Micro Cilantro

Chicken & Swiss Chard Ravioli

Butternut Squash Arancini with Parmesan Fondue

Diane Bush's Chile con Queso

Memories of Florence Duck Liver Croutons

Braised Beef Short Rib Sliders

Pulled Pork in Corn Muffin Cups

AMISTA VINEYARDS

Who could have imagined that a 2007 class project to make a bubbly from our rosé would lead us to sparkling wine production? The dry, sparkling Syrah was so delicious that we decided to make it ourselves, and it became the first estate sparkling wine from Dry Creek Valley. We're now on a quest to show that bubbles make every occasion special and go with all kinds of foods – especially these tartlets.

3320 Dry Creek Road | Healdsburg, CA 95448
707-431-9200
amistavineyards.com

CURRIED

CHICKEN TARTLETS

Pair with Amista Morningsong Vineyards Dry Creek Valley Sparkling Syrah

SERVES 12

CHICKEN SALAD

8 ounces golden raisins

1 cup Amista Sparking Syrah

2 pounds skinned, boneless chicken breasts, cooked and diced

2 cups celery, diced

1 cup sweet onion, diced

3 cups Fuji apples, peeled and diced

2 tablespoons curry powder

kosher salt and white pepper, to taste

8 ounces Major Grey chutney (mangoes with ginger)

4 ounces mayonnaise

1 cup micro greens

TARTLET SHELLS

1 pound bread flour

2 teaspoons baking powder

½ ounce salt

1 teaspoon sugar

4 ounces cold sweet cream butter, cut into cubes

1 egg

8 ounces milk

Start the recipe the night before you plan to serve the tartlets by preparing the tartlet dough and soaking the golden raisins overnight in the sparkling Syrah.

To make the dough, combine all the dry ingredients in a mixing bowl. Cut the butter into the dry mix with a pastry cutter, until the butter becomes crumbly. Mix in the egg and milk and stir to fully incorporate the ingredients. Knead the dough until it's smooth. Shape the dough into a log about the diameter of 1-½ inches, cover it with plastic wrap and refrigerate overnight, along with the soaking raisins.

The next day, preheat the oven to 350°. Cut the dough log into ½-inch-thick slices and roll them out so that they fit in your mini tart mold. Using your fingers, press the dough into the mold cups, and trim the excess dough with a small knife. Place another tart mold on top of the filled one and bake the shells upside down on a sheet pan until they turn golden brown. Let the shells cool, and then store them in a dry place until it's time to fill them with the chicken salad.

To prepare the salad, place the chicken, celery, onion and in a large bowl and mix well. Drain the soaked raisins (saving the liquid) and add them to the bowl. Sprinkle the curry powder, salt and pepper over the mixture and add the chutney. Toss the ingredients with a large spoon. In a small bowl, mix the raisin soaking liquid and mayonnaise, and add to the salad. Refrigerate for at least 4 hours.

To serve, fill each baked tartlet shell with a spoonful of the salad, topping them with a light dollop of chutney and micro greens.

CELLARS OF SONOMA

Elegant yet fun, this is a perfect appetizer for any party. A spicy beet surprise is surrounded by lush, molten goat cheese and finished with a salty-lemony crust. The dish looks beautiful and tastes even better!

133 Fourth Street | Santa Rosa, CA 95405
707-578-1826
cellarsofsonoma.com

GOLDEN BEET CROQUETTES
WITH MEYER LEMON SALT

Pair with Amorosa Bella Russian River Valley Chardonnay

MAKES 32

CROQUETTES

1 pound fresh goat cheese

1 large bunch golden beets, peeled and diced

1 cup water

¼ cup crisp white wine

juice of 1 orange

juice of 1 lemon

½ teaspoon fennel seed

½ teaspoon kosher salt

¼ teaspoon red pepper flakes

1 bay leaf

canola or peanut oil for frying

BREADING

1 cup flour

3 eggs, beaten with ½ teaspoon water

3 cups panko bread crumbs

LEMON SALT

2 tablespoons kosher salt

1 teaspoon sugar

zest of 1 Meyer lemon

Remove the goat cheese from the refrigerator and let it soften on the counter. Square off all the edges to make a perfect cube; be sure to remove any skin. Dice the cheese into ¼-inch cubes.

Place the diced beets, water, wine, orange and lemon juices, fennel seed, salt, red pepper flakes and bay leaf into a small stainless steel saucepan. Heat the mixture on low for 10 minutes, or until the beets are tender. Strain the beets and allow them to cool. Discard the liquid and bay leaf.

Form 1 tablespoon of goat cheese into balls and stuff the cooled beets into the center of each ball. Roll them in your hands to reshape, and refrigerate the balls until they're firm.

To prepare the breading, place the flour, beaten eggs and bread crumbs in separate bowls. Roll the goat cheese balls first in the flour (making sure to dust off any excess flour), then in the eggs to fully coat the balls, and then into the bread crumbs. You want a uniform coating. Return the balls to the refrigerator until you're ready to fry them.

In a deep fryer or large Dutch oven, heat the oil to 350°.

Remove the balls from the refrigerator. Prepare the lemon salt by mixing the salt, sugar and Meyer lemon zest into the bowl with the goat cheese balls. Use your fingertips to rub the salt on the surface of the balls. Fry them in small batches until they're golden brown, removing them to drain on paper towels.

Season the croquettes right away with the lemon salt and serve – perhaps on a nest of sunflower shoots.

FRANCIS FORD COPPOLA WINERY

Drawing on a life that has taken him around the world, Francis Ford Coppola shares his personal collection of recipes at Rustic, Francis' Favorites restaurant at the winery. A focal point of the dining room is the *parrilla* ("pah-REE-yah"), an authentic Argentine grill for cooking meats such as the New York steak in this recipe. But you don't need a *parrilla* to make this appetizer; a gas grill or Weber kettle will do just fine.

300 Via Archimedes | Geyserville, CA 95441
707-857-1485
franciscoppolawinery.com

PARRILLA-GRILLED NEW YORK STEAK
WITH ROMESCO & BRAISED MUSHROOMS

Pair with Francis Ford Coppola Director's Cut Cabernet Sauvignon

SERVES 4

ROMESCO SAUCE

1 red bell pepper

1 tomato, halved and seeded

2 cloves garlic

¼ cup olive oil

10 hazelnuts, shelled

10 peanuts, shelled

1 slice white bread

1 tablespoon sherry vinegar

STEAK

1 tablespoon olive oil

1 pound white button
    mushrooms, small

1 tablespoon garlic, slivered

2 glasses Director's Cut
    Cabernet Sauvignon

salt

black pepper

1 pound New York strip steak

Preheat oven to 300°.

Make the romesco sauce by roasting the pepper and tomato until their skins blacken. Peel the pepper and tomato and place them in a blender. In a small saucepan, slowly brown the whole garlic cloves in the oil until they're golden brown. Add the cloves and oil to the blender.

Toast the nuts and bread in the oven until they're golden brown and add them to the blender. Puree the mixture, add the vinegar, and season to taste with salt and pepper. Set the sauce aside.

To prepare the steak, add enough olive oil to coat the interior of a wide-bottomed skillet (approximately 1 tablespoon) and add the mushrooms and slivered garlic. Cook until the mushrooms are soft. Deglaze the pan with the wine and reduce by ½. Season the mushrooms to taste with salt and pepper and set them aside.

Season both sides of the steak with salt and pepper and grill it over a barbecue until its medium rare. Let the steak rest to retain the juices, and slice it into 8 pieces. Assemble the plate by placing a few mushrooms down first, then place the beef on top, and garnish with a dollop of romesco sauce.

HARVEST MOON ESTATE & WINERY

Duroc is a breed of pig prized for the quality and flavor of its meat. Pork tenderloin, the leanest and most tender cut, can also quickly dry out during cooking. To prevent that, chef Tim Vallery gives Duroc tenderloin a brine bath to ensure juiciness and full flavor. Brine the pork the day before you plan to cook it.

2192 Olivet Road | Santa Rosa, CA 95401
707-573-8711
harvestmoonwinery.com

SMOKED DUROC
PORK TENDERLOIN
WITH PORCINI FLAN

Pair with Harvest Moon Russian River Valley Pinot Noir

SERVES 12

PORK

3 pounds Duroc pork tenderloin, trimmed of fat and silver skin

1 cup water

1 cup Harvest Moon Pinot Noir

1-½ ounces brown sugar

1-½ ounces granulated sugar

6 ounces kosher salt

1 bunch thyme

2 bay leaves

1-¼ pounds ice

FLAN

2 ounces dried porcini mushrooms

¾ cup water

1-½ tablespoons olive oil

¼ cup yellow onion, minced

3 cloves garlic, minced

2 teaspoons thyme, finely chopped

1-½ cups heavy cream

4 egg yolks

pinch freshly grated nutmeg

pinch kosher salt

pinch freshly ground black pepper

½ cup Vella Dry Jack cheese

To prepare the pork, place in a stainless steel pan all of the ingredients except the ice and heat to 180°, stirring until all the ingredients are dissolved. Remove the pan from the heat and add the ice. Allow the pork loin to cool, then completely cover the pan and let the pork luxuriate in the brine for 6-24 hours.

Remove the meat from the brine and dry it completely with paper towels. Generously season the pork with salt and pepper. In a smoker using oak or hickory, indirectly smoke the tenderloin until an internal temperature of 145° is reached. Chill for at least 2 hours.

To prepare the flan, coat a ceramic baking dish with nonstick spray. Rinse the dried porcini mushrooms under cold running water. Place them in a saucepan with the fresh water and simmer until the mushrooms are soft. Strain the liquid and reserve it and the porcinis.

Preheat oven to 350°.

In a small saucepan, add the olive oil over medium heat. Add the onions and sauté them until they soften, about 3 minutes. Add the garlic and thyme and sauté for another minute. Transfer the mixture to the bowl of a food processor and add the reserved mushroom liquid and porcinis. Process until smooth.

In a bowl, mix the heavy cream, egg yolks, nutmeg, salt, pepper and cheese. Slowly whisk in the pureed mushroom mixture. Pour the flan into the ceramic dish and bake it in a water bath for 35-40 minutes, or until the center is firm.

To serve, cut the pork tenderloin in medallions and serve with the flan.

HAWLEY WINERY

We chose this recipe because it uses fresh, organic ingredients, which include goat cheese, basil and strawberries. It also makes wonderful hors d'oeuvres for parties and is a great alternative to sushi.

36 North Street | Healdsburg, CA 95448
707-473-9500
hawleywine.com

PROSCIUTTO 'MAKI ROLL'

Pair with Hawley Zinfandel

SERVES 4

4 ounces prosciutto, sliced

8 ounces fresh goat cheese, softened

1 bunch basil, stems and flowers removed

1 pint whole strawberries, tops removed

2 ounces extra virgin olive oil

1 ounce aged balsamic vinegar

Place the prosciutto slices on a large piece of parchment paper, overlapping the slices lengthwise in the approximate shape of an 8-inch by 10-inch rectangle (you will need 6-7 slices side by side).

Using a rubber spatula, spread a generous layer of goat cheese on the bottom ½ (5 inches x 8 inches) of the prosciutto. Arrange the basil leaves lengthwise down the center of the goat cheese. Arrange the whole strawberries on top of the basil, alternating directions so that they fit tightly together.

Using the parchment paper, tightly roll the prosciutto as you would a maki sushi roll; use the upper exposed portion of the prosciutto to seal the roll. Refrigerate the rolls for 15-20 minutes.

Carefully slice through the center of each strawberry; you will be able to feel for the center of the berries with your index finger. Slice into approximately 1-inch-thick pieces, arrange them on a platter and finish with a drizzle of extra virgin olive oil. Serve the rolls with aged balsamic vinegar for dipping.

HOLDREDGE WINES

If there is one thing that identifies classic Italian cuisine, it is that the very best dishes often have the fewest ingredients. "Four ingredients maximum" is a phrase heard often in Italian kitchens – "*Quattro ingredienti massima.*"
Use the freshest ingredients and let them speak. This recipe is a favorite for us at the holidays. We splurge (when we can afford it) on fresh truffles from Italy, and truffle oil is a workhorse substitute. We dip hunks of warm crusty bread into it, and it pairs beautifully with Pinot Noir.

51 Front Street | Healdsburg, CA 95448
707-431-1424
holdredge.com

VEGI

CLASSIC ITALIAN

FONDUTA CON TARTUFI

(FONDUE WITH TRUFFLES)

Pair with Holdredge Russian River Valley Pinot Noir

SERVES 8

2 cups heavy cream

½ pound fontina cheese

¼- to ½-ounce fresh truffles, or 1 tablespoon truffle oil

1 loaf crusty bread, warm

In a double boiler, heat the cream over medium heat, stirring regularly. Before it begins to scald, add the fontina. If it is too thick, thin the sauce with a little bit of milk.

Remove the fondue from the heat (it will thicken as it cools). Shave razor-thin slices of fresh truffles into the fondue, or add the truffle oil. Stir and serve — *molto delizioso!*

INSPIRATION VINEYARDS & WINERY

When we moved to Sonoma County in 2001 to start our winery, the 100-year-old Zinfandel vines in the "front yard" had never been used to make a single-vineyard wine. After our first commercial harvest of 2002, we discovered what a gem we had with this old vineyard, as it produced a wine that was savory and spicy — white pepper, cardamom, bay and cloves. We tell folks it's a spice rack in a bottle, and when you pair it with something that has rosemary and black pepper, it's a symphony of flavors, both complementary and contrasting.

3360 Coffey Lane, Suite E | Santa Rosa, CA 95403
707-237-4980
inspirationvineyards.com

GRILLED ROSEMARY STEAK SKEWERS
WITH PARMESAN SAUCE

Pair with Inspiration Vineyards Russian River Valley Old Vine Zinfandel

SERVES 8

½ cup Parmesan cheese, grated

½ cup sour cream

2 tablespoons whipping cream

1 tablespoon fresh lemon juice

1 teaspoon prepared horseradish

1 teaspoon kosher salt, divided

1-¼ teaspoons ground black pepper, divided

1-½ pounds top sirloin or New York steak, trimmed and cut diagonally into ½-inch strips

4 tablespoons extra virgin olive oil

2 tablespoons fresh rosemary, chopped

1 tablespoon garlic puree

In a small bowl, combine the cheese, sour cream, whipping cream, lemon juice, horseradish, ¼ teaspoon of the salt and ¾ teaspoon of the pepper. Set the bowl aside.

Thread the steak strips onto metal skewers, 1 strip per skewer.

Combine the olive oil, rosemary and garlic puree in a bowl, and brush both sides of the meat with this mixture. Sprinkle the steak with the remaining salt and pepper.

Prepare a grill to medium-high heat. Place the skewers on the grill and cook the steak to desired doneness, about 2-1/2 minutes per side for medium. Remove the steak from the grill and let it rest, loosely covered with foil, for 5 minutes.

Serve the steak with the reserved Parmesan sauce.

KELLEY & YOUNG WINES

Who doesn't like pulled pork? I developed this
recipe as a take on my "to die for" baby back ribs.
It has all the flavor of the ribs but no bones,
is not as messy, and is just so easy to make.

428 Hudson Street | Healdsburg, CA 95448
707-433-2364
kelleyyoungwines.com

SLOW-ROASTED ITALIAN
PULLED PORK
WITH ZINFANDEL BBQ SAUCE

Pair with Kelley & Young Alexander Valley Zinfandel

SERVES 15-20

PORK

3-½ to 4-pound pork shoulder roast

olive oil

3–4 twigs rosemary, stripped and chopped

1 small garlic head, crushed and chopped

salt, to taste

pepper, to taste

BBQ SAUCE

olive oil

3-4 cloves garlic, crushed and chopped

1-½ cups Kelley & Young Zinfandel

1 cup ketchup

¼ cup soy sauce

¼ cup Worcestershire sauce

½ cup brown sugar

Preheat oven to 450° or it's highest setting.

To prepare the pork, coat the roast with olive oil and smear it with the rosemary, garlic, salt and pepper. Place the pork in a heavy roasting pan and roast in the oven 40 minutes, or until the edges of the meat start to caramelize. Cover the pan tightly, turn down the oven to 325°, and continue to roast for 2 hours or until the meat is falling apart.

While the roast cooks, prepare the barbecue sauce. Place the oil in a medium saucepan over medium heat. Add the garlic and cook for 1 minute. Add the Zinfandel and cook to reduce to about ½, 10-15 minutes. Add the remaining ingredients and stir frequently to prevent scorching. Cook until the sauce reaches the desired thickness, 30–40 minutes.

Shred the meat when it is cool enough handle. Serve it on small squares of bread (I like to use soft rosemary focaccia) topped with the BBQ sauce and a sprig of tender rosemary leaves, crispy garlic or chives.

LONGBOARD VINEYARDS

Michael Phillips had no problem at all impressing us with his food at Island Style Deli in Bodega Bay. His Hawaiian-style cuisine is both delicious and a natural fit for our Surf Lounge (particularly since winemaker Oded Shakked is partial to surfing and surf food). It was Michael's Kahlua Pork Sliders that won over the Longboard ladies, leaving us no doubt as to what to share with our guests over a glass of Syrah. You can find the banana leaves at Asian markets.

5 Fitch Street | Healdsburg, CA 95448
707-433-3473
longboardvineyards.com

DAKINE KAHLUA
PORK SLIDERS

Pair with Longboard Russian River Valley Syrah

SERVES 40

PORK

1 medium pork butt

20 cloves garlic, minced

⅛ cup Hawaiian sea salt

2 tablespoons coarse black pepper

banana leaves, enough to cover
   the pork

¼ cup pineapple juice

¼ cup chicken stock

2 tablespoons liquid smoke

⅛ cup soy sauce

¼ cup Longboard Syrah

King's Hawaiian Sweet Rolls

PINEAPPLE SLAW

2 cups crushed pineapple

½ cup Best Foods mayonnaise

3 tablespoons sweet rice vinegar

¼ cup sugar

salt, to taste

pepper, to taste

BARBECUE SAUCE

2 cups ketchup

¼ cup passion fruit or strawberry jelly

¼ cup pineapple juice

¼ cup brown sugar

2 tablespoons soy sauce

1 teaspoon liquid smoke

⅛ cup Longboard Syrah

Preheat oven to 275°.

Season the pork butt with garlic, Hawaiian salt and black pepper. Wrap the pork in banana leaves, then cover it with foil. Place the pork in a roasting pan. Add the pineapple juice, chicken stock, liquid smoke, soy sauce and Syrah to the bottom of the pan. Cover the entire pan with foil and place it in the preheated oven for 6 hours.

To prepare the pineapple slaw, mix all the ingredients in a medium bowl. Cover the bowl and place it in the refrigerator until the pork is ready to serve.

To prepare the barbecue sauce, place all the ingredients in a medium bowl and mix well. Set the sauce aside until you are ready to serve the sliders.

When the pork has cooked for 6 hours, remove the foil and banana leaves. Let it cool slightly, then shred the meat with 2 forks. Place a spoonful of the pork on the bottom ½ of each Hawaiian roll and top with a dollop each of the barbeque sauce and pineapple slaw.

LOST CANYON WINERY

I first tasted a Croque Madame at a little bistro in San Francisco. I lived in the Financial district for years and one particular morning after a long night on the cooking line and a few drinks the night before, I woke up with a throbbing head and a hankering for something rich and delicious to ease my pain. I walked to a little alley called Belden Place, where you feel instantly transported to a small European neighborhood. I went to Plouf, a French bistro on the alley, and had a grilled ham and cheese sandwich dipped in French toast batter and topped with a fried egg. Wow! I was cured. This is my appetizer-sized version of that sandwich: a wine country ham and cheese.

123 Fourth Street | Santa Rosa, CA 95401
707-623-9621
lostcanyonwinery.com

TRUFFLED CROQUE MADAME
WITH QUAIL EGG

Pair with Lost Canyon Whitton Vineyard Russian River Valley Pinot Noir

SERVES 4

¼ pound unsalted butter, divided

2 tablespoons all-purpose flour

¼ cup buttery Chardonnay

1 cup half and half, divided

1 tablespoon Dijon mustard

salt and pepper, to taste

2 dashes nutmeg

½ yellow onion, thinly sliced

1 chicken egg

2 slices Costeaux sourdough bread

4 slices truffled Sottocenere cheese

1-½ slices honey baked ham

4 quail eggs

Melt ½ of the butter in a small saucepan. Whisk in the flour and cook over medium-low heat for 5 minutes. Add the Chardonnay while whisking and cook until the sauce is thick, about 2 minutes.

Add to the saucepan ½ cup of the half and half and continue to whisk, adding the mustard, salt, pepper and 1 dash of nutmeg. Set the pan aside to cool.

Melt 2 tablespoons of butter in a small sauté pan and add the onions. Cook them for approximately 20 minutes, until they're soft and the color of a penny.

In a shallow bowl, mix the remaining half and half, 1 dash of nutmeg, the chicken egg and a pinch of salt. Combine well with a whisk and set it aside.

To build the sandwich, place both slices of bread next to one another. Spread them with the Chardonnay sauce and add the cheese on each slice, the ham and caramelized onions on the other. Put the bread slices together.

Dip the sandwich on both sides in the egg batter and shake it to remove the excess. In a skillet over medium-heat, melt 2 tablespoons of butter until they completely met and the foam dissipates. Place the battered sandwich in the skillet, cover it with a lid or metal bowl, and cook for about 3 minutes, until the bottom is golden. Using a spatula, flip the sandwich and cook the other side until golden, 2-3 minutes.

Remove the sandwich from the skillet and let it rest for a few minutes. Melt the remaining butter over medium heat. Crack the quail eggs into separate corners of the skillet and cook until their whites are firm. Trim the crust from the sandwich with a serrated knife, quarter it and top each piece with a quail egg.

MAZZOCCO SONOMA

When winemaker Antoine Favero's delicious Zinfandel pairs with Radio Africa & Kitchen chef Eskender Aseged's superbly prepared lamb, magic happens. The wine's spicy pepper and rich, dark berry notes bring out the seductive savory qualities of this satisfying dish.

1400 Lytton Springs Road | Healdsburg, CA 95448
707-431-8159
mazzocco.com

LAMB CROSTINI
WITH CHERMOULA AIOLI

Pair with Mazzocco Seaton Zinfandel

SERVES 12

CHERMOULA

½ cup lemon juice

3 tablespoons paprika

½ teaspoon cayenne

3 tablespoons garlic

3 tablespoons parsley, chopped

3 teaspoons cumin

3 tablespoons olive oil

3 teaspoons ground coriander

¾ cup organic mayonnaise

LAMB

2 pounds leg of lamb, cut and
   trimmed into loin-style pieces

CROSTINI

1 long, thick, sweet baguette

3-4 tablespoons parsley,
   chopped

Mix all of the chermoula ingredients except for the mayonnaise in a bowl. Marinate the lamb in ⅓ of the chermoula for 20 minutes or up to 2 hours.

Whisk the remaining chermoula with the mayonnaise to create a chermoula aioli. Set it aside.

Preheat a grill and preheat the oven to 350°.

Cut the baguette into ½-inch slices and toast them in the oven for 4 minutes.

Grill the lamb, alternating sides, until the meat is medium rare, about 6 minutes. Let the meat rest for 2 minutes and then cut it into thin slices.

To serve, place the lamb slices on top of the toasted baguette slices, drizzle with chermoula aioli and sprinkle the chopped parsley on top.

RODNEY STRONG VINEYARDS

King salmon, also known as Chinook, is native to Northern California and Alaskan waterways. Winemaker Rick Sayre is an avid fan of fishing for salmon and crafts a fine Pinot Noir to accompany the delicious fish. The subtle combination of peppers, Dijon mustard and fresh salmon make for an unforgettable pairing.

11455 Old Redwood Highway | Healdsburg, CA 95448
707-431-1533
rodneystrong.com

KING SALMON CAKES

Pair with Rodney Strong Russian River Valley Reserve Pinot Noir

SERVES 20

2 pounds wild king salmon, skin off, pin bones out, ¼-inch dice

4 ounces smoked salmon, ¼-inch dice

¼ cup garlic, minced

¼ cup yellow bell pepper, fine dice

¼ cup red bell pepper, fine dice

¼ cup fennel, fine dice

¼ cup red onion, fine dice

¼ cup carrot, shredded and minced

2 tablespoons fennel fronds, fine chopped

2 tablespoons fresh dill, fine chopped

1 whole egg

1 egg white

2 tablespoons Dijon mustard

2 tablespoons mayonnaise

1 cup panko bread crumbs

1 tablespoon kosher salt

1 tablespoon olive oil

In a large bowl, combine all the ingredients except for the olive oil and blend well. Form 3-ounce patties from the mixture.

Heat a nonstick pan over medium-high heat. Add 1 tablespoon of olive oil and sear the salmon cakes on both sides, about 2 minutes per side.

These cakes are a great as both an appetizer and an entrée.

ROUTE 128 WINERY

Since fulfilling our dream of creating Route 128 Winery, our nephew and professional chef Rian Rinn has been at the center of our delicious food and wine pairings. Now Rian is living his dream, using his years of culinary and butchering experience to open the Sonoma County Meat Co. in late 2013. Hearty cheers to Rian! Now some of our fans will have regular access to the delicious sausages Rian creates for us. Seafood is another of his areas of expertise, as demonstrated by this shrimp appetizer. You'll need a vacuum food sealer to make this at home.

21079 Geyserville Avenue | Geyserville, CA 95441
707-696-0004
route128winery.com

SHRIMP ON A STICK

WITH 'INFLATED' WILD RICE

Pair with Route 128 Alexander Valley Syrah

SERVES 6-8

GLAZE

½ bottle Route 128 Syrah

½ cup sugar

⅓ cup white corn syrup

SHRIMP

1 pound shrimp, peeled
  (16 count)

15 thick bamboo skewers

3 tablespoons butter

1 tablespoon allspice berries,
  whole

1 teaspoon juniper berries

3 whole bay leaves

½ bunch fresh thyme

3 whole jalapeno chiles,
  cut in ½ lengthwise

3 large lemon peels

1-½ cups Route 128 Viognier

3 teaspoons salt

2 large shallots, sliced

RICE

2 cups peanut or other frying oil

¾ cup wild rice

salt, to taste

1 teaspoon oregano powder

To prepare the glaze, combine the Syrah, sugar and white corn syrup in a small pan over medium heat. Cook the mixture until it is reduced by ⅔ and set the pan aside.

To prepare the shrimp, uncurl them and flatten them with your palm. Skewer each shrimp, starting with the tail and pushing the skewer into the body (but not all the way through it), 1 shrimp per skewer. Place 5 skewers in each of 3 vacuum-seal bags.

Also place in each bag ⅓ of the butter, allspice and juniper berries, bay leaves, thyme, jalapenos, lemon peels, Viognier, salt and shallots, Vacuum-seal the bags, making sure there is no air in them. Place enough water in a large pot to cover the 3 bags completely. Heat the water to 175°. Place the bags in the water for 9 minutes and keep the temperature at 175°.

While the shrimp cook, prepare the wild rice. Heat the peanut oil in a wide sauté pan to the smoking point. Add the grains and stir rapidly and continuously, cooking only until the grains plump yet don't burst, approximately 2 minutes. Remove the pan from the heat, season the wild rice with salt and oregano powder, and cover with foil to keep it warm.

After 9 minutes of cooking, remove the bags from the pot and remove the skewered shrimp from the bags (discard the remaining contents). Place the skewers on a platter, side by side. Pat the shrimp dry and drizzle the Syrah glaze over them. Then sprinkle a liberal amount of the plumped wild rice over the glaze, so that the rice adheres to the shrimp. Serve immediately.

RUSSIAN RIVER VINEYARDS

I visited the Paisano Brothers Fishery in Bodega Bay last fall, and dockmaster Richie, a great family friend, had just had a wild tuna come in from a boat. He asked if I wanted to take it home and prepare a dish for a barbecue we had planned that day for friends and family. This is what I came up with for an appetizer – and it was a show stopper, loved by all.

5700 Gravenstein Highway North | Forestville, CA 95436
707-887-3344
russianrivervineyards.com

AHH-HEE TUNA & AVOCADO SALAD
ON ENDIVE

Pair with Russian River Vineyards Pinot Noir

SERVES 20

1 line-caught, sushi-grade ahi tuna

2 Hass avocados

2 tablespoons sesame oil

juice of 2 limes

zest of 1 lime

salt and pepper, to taste

20 endive leaves

1 pint cream

¼ teaspoon fresh wasabi, grated

1 tablespoon sesame seeds, toasted

15 shiso leaves, cut into ribbons

Dice the ahi and avocados into ¼-inch squares. Place them in a medium bowl and add to it the sesame oil, lime juice, lime zest, salt and pepper. Place dollops of the tuna mixture on the end of each endive leaf.

In a clean bowl, whisk the cream until it has the consistency to coat the back of a spoon. Whisk in the wasabi, and drizzle the mixture over the ahi and avocado on the endive. Garnish with sesame seeds and a shiso leaf ribbon.

SAPPHIRE HILL WINERY

We love ahi tuna in a variety of ways: cooked over an open flame, as sashimi, and as tartare. This version is a wonderful appetizer, guaranteed to be a hit with your friends. If you don't have time to fry the wontons, bake them in the oven.

55 Front Street | Healdsburg, CA 95448
707-431-1888
sapphirehill.com

POISSON CRU AHI CONES
WITH MICRO CILANTRO

Pair with Sapphire Hill Russian River Valley Chardonnay

SERVES 6

⅓ pound sashimi-grade ahi tuna

juice of 3 limes

salt to taste

½ jalapeno, seeded and diced

½ medium Maui or other sweet yellow onion, diced

½ cup coconut milk

1 tablespoon cilantro, cut into thin ribbons

canola oil for frying

6 round wonton wrappers

vegetable spray

1 egg mixed with 1 tablespoon water, beaten

⅓ cup micro cilantro

1 tablespoon olive oil

1 tablespoon black sesame seeds, for garnish

1 tablespoon white sesame seeds, for garnish

In a large bowl, combine the tuna and lime juice. Season the fish with salt, wait 2 minutes, and add the jalapeno, onion, coconut milk and cilantro ribbons. Mix to combine.

Add to a wide pot or deep fryer enough oil to be a least 2 inches deep. Heat the oil to 350°.

Roll a piece of tin foil into a cone shape by wrapping it around a cylinder and folding it in. Spray the foil with vegetable spray. Wrap each wonton wrapper around the foil to form a cone. Seal the cones with the egg wash.

Once at a time, place the wrapped cylinders into the hot oil and fry until they're golden brown, turning them as necessary. Remove the cones from the oil and place them on a paper towel-lined tray. Season them lightly with salt.

In a small bowl, toss the micro cilantro with the olive oil and a bit of juice from the tuna. Fill the cones with the ahi mixture, and top each with the cilantro and sesame seeds, and serve.

SBRAGIA FAMILY VINEYARDS

These ravioli are quite versatile, as they can complement white and red wines, depending on the type of sauce you serve with them. Here, wild and farmed mushrooms are the foundation for a sauce that matches beautifully with our Home Ranch Chardonnay.

9990 Dry Creek Road | Geyserville, CA 95441
707-473-2992
sbragia.com

CHICKEN & SWISS CHARD

RAVIOLI

Pair with Sbragia Family Vineyards Home Ranch Chardonnay

MAKES 40 RAVIOLI

RAVIOLI

1-½ cups Swiss chard, salted, steamed, squeezed and chopped fine

¾ pound chicken breasts, boneless and skinless

salt and pepper, to taste

1 tablespoon olive oil

1 pound ricotta cheese (excellent quality)

½ teaspoon white pepper

1 cup Parmesan cheese, grated

¼ teaspoon nutmeg, grated

3 eggs, beaten

40 wonton wrappers, 3 to 4 inches round

MUSHROOM SAUCE

1 medium onion, finely minced

2 tablespoons garlic, chopped

2 ounces butter

2 ounces olive oil

1 pound assorted wild and farmed mushrooms, cleaned and sliced

salt and pepper, to taste

1 tablespoon fresh thyme, chopped

½ cup Chardonnay

½ cup broth (mushroom or chicken)

½ cup heavy cream

1 cup Parmesan cheese, freshly ground

3 tablespoons Italian parsley, chopped

To prepare the ravioli, first make sure that you drain all the excess liquid from the chard; otherwise, the ravioli filling will be too loose.

Season the chicken breasts with salt and pepper and rub them with olive oil. Place the pieces in a sauté pan over medium heat and cook the breasts until they're just done. Remove them from the pan and let them cool. Chop the chicken into large chunks and place them in a food processor, pulsing them to a finely ground mixture but with still a little texture left.

In a medium bowl, mix thoroughly the ricotta, white pepper, Parmesan, nutmeg and beaten eggs. Season the mixture with salt and pepper, if needed.

To fill the ravioli, place a teaspoon of the chicken mixture into the center of 20 of the wonton wrappers. Place the remaining wrappers on top of the filling and press around all the edges to seal the filling. Cook the ravioli in boiling water for 2 minutes after the pasta pieces begin to float to the top.

Sauté the onions and garlic in the olive oil and butter until they're golden. Add the mushrooms, salt, pepper and thyme. Cook over medium heat, covered, for 5 minutes. Add Chardonnay to the pan and simmer the mixture, uncovered, until it's almost evaporated. Add the broth and cream, stir, and continue to simmer the sauce until it thickens slightly. Add the Parmesan.

Taste and adjust the seasonings. Pour the sauce over the hot ravioli and garnish with the parsley.

SONOMA-CUTRER VINEYARDS

Arancini are deep-fried risotto balls that are said to have originated in Sicily. They can be customized with various fillings and served with different sauces; in this version, butternut squash is the star ingredient, and a creamy Parmesan fondue is the sauce. To make this recipe vegetarian, substitute vegetable stock for the chicken stock.

4401 Slusser Road | Windsor, CA 95492
707-237-3489
sonomacutrer.com

BUTTERNUT SQUASH ARANCINI
WITH PARMESAN FONDUE

Pair with Sonoma-Cutrer Russian River Valley Pinot Noir

SERVES 4

1 butternut squash

4 cups chicken stock

2 tablespoons olive oil

1 small yellow onion, diced

1-½ cups carnaroli rice

½ cup white wine

1 cup Parmesan cheese, grated

2 cups cream

8 ounces fresh mozzarella cheese, cut into ¼-inch pieces

salt and pepper

1 cup all-purpose flour

4 eggs, beaten

2 cups panko bread crumbs

4-6 quarts rice bran or canola oil, for frying

Preheat oven to 350°.

Slice the butternut squash in ½ lengthwise and remove the seeds. Place the halves, skin side up, on a sheet pan lined with parchment paper. Roast the squash in the oven for 45-60 minutes, until it's soft. Remove the pan from the oven and let the squash cool.

Peel off the skin of the squash, place the flesh in a food processor, and blend until it's smooth.

To prepare the risotto, place the chicken stock and ½ of the squash puree in a pot on the stove, and bring the contents to a simmer.

Place the olive oil and onions in a skillet over medium heat, and sweat the onions until they're translucent. Add the rice and continue to cook 2-3 minutes, until the rice is translucent. Add the wine, cook for 2-3 minutes, and begin adding the hot chicken-squash mixture to the rice, 1 cup at a time. Add more once the liquid is almost gone, and continue this process until the risotto is tender. Fold in the rest of the butternut puree.

Spread the risotto evenly on a ½-sheet pan and allow it to cool.

Meanwhile, to prepare the fondue, combine the Parmesan and cream in a heavy pot. Bring the liquid to a boil and turn off the heat. Let the mixture sit for 30 minutes. Strain the cheese out of the cream and transfer the cream to a clean pot (discard the cheese). Bring the cream to a boil and reduce it over medium-low heat until the cream thickens enough to cover the back of a spoon. Keep the fondue warm.

Scoop the risotto into balls. Place a piece of mozzarella in the center of each ball and shape it round with your hands. Set up a breading station with 3 bowls: 1 with flour seasoned with salt and pepper, 1 bowl with the whisked eggs and 1 with the bread crumbs seasoned with salt and pepper.

Take each risotto ball and dip it into the flour, then the egg and finally the bread crumbs. Place them on sheet pan.

Heat a heavy pot and add to it 6 inches of oil. Heat the oil to 350° and place 6-8 arancini in the oil at a time. Fry them until they're golden brown, 3-4 minutes. Cook all the arancini in batches, and season them with salt and pepper while they're hot. Place the warm fondue on a serving platter and arrange the arancini on top of the fondue. Garnish with shaved Parmesan and serve.

STEPHEN & WALKER WINERY

This recipe comes from Tony's mother, Diane Bush. I first tasted this dish 33 years ago at a family gathering, and it has been one of my favorite things to serve and share with friends and family. We eat this right from the pot, in the kitchen, with kids, dogs and friends running through the house. Celebrate with your own family with this crowd-pleasing appetizer.

243 Healdsburg Avenue | Healdsburg, CA 95448
707-431-8749
trustwine.com

DIANE BUSH'S

CHILE CON QUESO

Pair with Stephen & Walker Trust Winery Limited Pinot Noir

SERVES 40

4 tablespoons olive oil

2 cups yellow onions, diced

4 8-ounce cans Anaheim chiles, diced

2 tablespoons flour

8 tomatoes, diced

2 16-ounce boxes Velveta cheese, cut into ½-inch cubes

½ cup evaporated milk

salt and pepper, to taste

In a very large Dutch oven or stock pot, sauté the onions in the olive oil over medium-high heat, until the onions are translucent and caramelized, about 15 minutes.

Add the chiles and sauté for another 10 minutes. Add the flour and stir to make a paste with the onions and chiles. Stir in the diced tomatoes.

Add the cheese cubes to the pot and reduce the heat to low. Stir continuously until the cheese is melted and bubbles very slowly. Use the evaporated milk to adjust the consistency if it's too thick.

Season with salt and pepper, and serve the dip with chips, bread, pretzels or vegetables.

TOPEL WINERY TASTING ROOM

One of my first, and lasting, memories of living in Florence, Italy, is this incredibly delicious appetizer! The bread is grilled over an open fire, rubbed with raw garlic, drizzled with just-pressed, slightly peppery olive oil, and topped with a duck liver mixture. Sublime.

125 Matheson Street | Healdsburg, CA 95448
707-433-4116
topelwines.com

MEMORIES OF FLORENCE

DUCK LIVER CROUTONS

Pair with Topel Sweetie Pie Zinfandel

MAKES 24 CROUTONS

3 ounces pancetta, cut into small bits

2 shallots, finely diced

2 tablespoons Sweetie Pie Zinfandel

3 tablespoons olive oil

12 ounces duck livers, veins and fat removed, lightly salted and peppered

1 clove garlic, mashed to a paste

2 tablespoons Topel extra virgin olive oil

¼ teaspoon salt

6 salt-packed anchovy filets, soaked in several changes of water, drained and chopped

1 tablespoon capers, soaked in several changes of cold water and drained

freshly ground black pepper

1 loaf sourdough bread

additional clove garlic for rubbing the bread

Add the pancetta to a sauté pan over medium heat and cook for about 1 minute, until the pancetta begins to render some of its fat. Add the shallots, lower the heat, and cook for 5 minutes, until the shallots have softened.

Add the Zinfandel and scrape up any bits adhering to the bottom of the pan. When the wine has evaporated, transfer the mixture to a plate and set it aside.

In the same pan, warm the 3 tablespoons of olive oil. Place the livers in the pan, side by side, and cook them over low heat for 3-4 minutes, turning them over every minute so as not to brown them. Transfer the livers to a plate when they become just firm throughout; they should remain pink in the center. Let the livers cool.

Coarsely chop the livers and combine them in a bowl with the shallots, pancetta and any juices from the plate they rested on. Add the garlic, extra virgin olive oil, salt, anchovies and capers. Grind black pepper over the ingredients and mix them well.

Grill slices of the sourdough bread until they're golden brown, then rub them with the remaining clove of raw garlic. Spread the liver mixture on top of the warm croutons and serve while still warm.

VML WINERY

After a harvest dinner party, we had some leftover braised short rib stew. The following day I brought fresh sourdough rolls to the winery, and the crew assembled sliders from the warmed meat. These afternoon delights are great when the days get colder and the last of the grapes are being harvested. Here's how we make the sliders from scratch.

4035 Westside Road | Healdsburg, CA 95448
707-431-4404
vmlwine.com

CHEF DAN LUCIA, DL CATERING

BRAISED BEEF
SHORT RIB SLIDERS

Pair with VML Floodgate Vineyard Pinot Noir

SERVES 8

SLIDERS

3 tablespoons olive oil

6 pounds beef short ribs

8 cups beef stock

⅓ cup carrot, chopped

⅓ cup celery, chopped

⅓ cup yellow onion, chopped

3 garlic cloves, chopped

1 cup aioli or mayonnaise

8 sourdough rolls, toasted

SLAW

1 cup olive oil

4 tablespoons Dijon mustard

3 tablespoons Champagne
   vinegar

juice of 2 lemons

4 cups green cabbage, shaved

1 cup red onion, shaved

salt and pepper, to taste

Preheat oven to 325°.

Place 3 tablespoons of olive oil in a sauté pan, turn the heat to high, and add the short ribs, searing them until they're nicely browned. Remove the ribs to a braising dish. Add to this dish the beef stock, carrot, celery, yellow onion and garlic. Cover the dish and place it in the preheated oven for approximately 4 hours, or until the meat is fall-off-the-bone tender. Let the beef cool and pull it apart with your hands or using 2 forks, keeping it in contact with the braising liquid. Set aside.

To prepare the slaw, add the olive oil, mustard, vinegar and lemon juice to a medium bowl. Mix well. Add the shaved cabbage and red onion, and toss the ingredients. Season with salt and pepper.

To assemble the sliders, reheat the shredded meat, toast the sourdough rolls, and spread aioli or mayonnaise on both halves of each roll. Spoon the meat onto the bottom bun and top with a dollop of the slaw.

WINDSOR VINEYARDS

We made this recipe for our hardworking cellar crew after one of the longest days during harvest. After a crazy day, what could be better than pulled pork and cornbread? Putting them together, of course! Any leftover pulled pork can be frozen for future enjoyment.

308 B Center Street | Healdsburg, CA 95448
707-921-2893
windsorvineyards.com

PULLED PORK
IN CORN MUFFIN CUPS

Pair with Windsor Vineyards Dry Creek Valley Zinfandel

MAKES 24 MINI MUFFINS

PORK

1 fresh pork shoulder,
    5-7 pounds

1 tablespoon salt

black pepper, to taste

1-¼ cups vinegar

2 tablespoons sugar

½ cup ketchup

½ cup barbecue sauce

1-½ tablespoons crushed red
    pepper flakes

dash of hot sauce

MUFFINS

3 cups all-purpose flour

⅔ cup sugar

1 cup medium-grind cornmeal

2 tablespoons baking powder

1-½ teaspoons salt

1 cup whole milk

½ cup heavy cream

½ pound unsalted butter,
    melted and cooled

2 extra-large eggs

To prepare the pulled pork, place the shoulder in a slow cooker. Sprinkle salt and pepper over the meat and add the vinegar. Cover the pot and cook on low heat for 9-12 hours.

Remove the pork from the pot and remove the meat from the bones, placing the meat in a mixing bowl. Strain the liquid, discard the excess fat, and keep approximately 2 cups of liquid. Place it and the remaining ingredients in the bowl with the pork and mix with a wooden spoon. Return the mixture to the crock pot, cover, and cook on low heat for 1-2 hours longer.

To prepare the muffins, preheat the oven to 350°. Place paper liners in the wells of a 24 mini-muffin pan and coat them with nonstick spray.

In the bowl of an electric mixer fitted with a paddle attachment, mix the flour, sugar, cornmeal, baking powder and salt. In a separate bowl, combine the milk, heavy cream, melted butter and eggs. With the mixer on the lowest speed, pour the wet ingredients into the dry ones and process until the mixture is just blended.

Spoon the batter into the paper liners, filling each one to the top. Bake for 12 minutes, until the tops are crisp and a toothpick comes out clean. Let the muffins cool slightly and remove them from the pan. Using a mini melon baller, scoop out the tops of the muffins.

To serve, fill the muffins with approximately 1 tablespoon of pork — and dig in!

SOUPS

Jene's 3x3x3 Harvest Chili

The Ultimate Lobster Bisque

Ryan's Romantic Rosemary & Bacon Beef Stew

Butternut Squash Bisque

Potato Bacon Soup

Carrot Potato Bisque With Roasted Pepper & Cilantro

Pork & Black Bean Stew

Wine Country Smoked Bacon & Lentil Soup

Black Bean Soup

Black Calypso Bean Soup with Ham Bone

Stracciatelle

Taft Street Crab Chowder

BLANCHARD FAMILY WINES

Since the birth of Blanchard Family Wines, Jene Chapanar has played many roles for us: winemaker, craftsman, mentor and even chef. This recipe is something he developed over the years to share with friends and family at parties, picnics and wine dinners. It's called 3x3x3 because it includes three beans, three chiles and three meats. We love it on a cold harvest night after a long day of crush, by the fire with a glass of our Zinfandel, but the dish is wonderful any time of year.

109 W. North Street | Healdsburg, CA 95448
630-606-4389
blanchardfamilywines.com

JENE'S 3X3X3 HARVEST
CHILI

Pair with Blanchard Family Wines Jackson James Zinfandel

SERVES 10-15

3 tablespoons butter

½ pound smoked bacon, cross-cut into ¼-inch slices

2 jalapeno chiles, diced

3 roasted poblano chiles, peeled and diced

2 red bell peppers, diced

2 red onions, diced

1 head garlic, minced

1 pound sirloin tips, cut into ½-inch cubes

1 pound hot Italian sausage

2 pounds 80/20 ground beef

2 tablespoons granulated garlic

2 tablespoons hot paprika

2 teaspoons cumin

2 teaspoons coriander

3 teaspoons chipotle powder

2 cans tomato sauce (Muir Glen preferred)

1 can fire-roasted tomatoes (Muir Glen)

2 cans kidney beans, with juice

2 cans white beans, with juice

2 cans garbanzos beans, with juice

½ bottle Zinfandel

chicken broth

In a large stock pot, melt the butter over medium heat. Add the bacon and cook down to render the fat.

Add the jalapeno and roasted poblano chiles, red bell pepper, garlic and onions, and cook until the vegetables are translucent. Remove them from the pot and set side.

Add the meats and brown them in batches. Return all the meat and the vegetables to the pot and add the spices (garlic, paprika, cumin, coriander and chipotle powder) and cook, stirring, for 1 minute. Add the tomato sauce and tomatoes; stir for 2 minutes. Add the beans, then the Zinfandel and enough chicken broth to cover everything. Simmer the chili for 2 hours. Season with salt and pepper to taste, and serve.

After browning the meat, you can also finish the chili in a crock pot.

DAVID COFFARO
VINEYARD & WINERY

We first served this delicious lobster bisque at the winery during a Barrel Tasting Weekend a few years ago. The sheer number of people fighting to the front of the line for seconds led us to believe this was the perfect recipe for our cookbook submission. Now you can enjoy this dish with your family and friends ... no elbowing necessary.

7485 Dry Creek Road | Geyserville, CA 95441
707-433-9715
coffaro.com

THE ULTIMATE
LOBSTER BISQUE

Pair with Coffaro Dry Creek Valley Sauvignon Blanc

SERVES 12

LOBSTER STOCK

5 pounds lobster shells

1 pound shrimp shells

2 whole carrots, peeled and cut into ¼-inch slices

1 yellow onion, diced large

1 bay leaf

1 bunch thyme

3 stalks celery, chopped into 1-inch pieces

BISQUE

¼ cup butter, divided

½ cup shallots, diced

6 cloves garlic, minced

1 small can San Marzano tomatoes, drained of juice

½ bottle Coffaro Sauvignon Blanc

½ gallon heavy cream

½ gallon lobster stock

1 tablespoon flour

1 ounce lemon juice

salt, to taste

red pepper flakes, to taste

½ pound lobster meat, finely chopped

1 ounce Meyer lemon olive oil

chives or tarragon, chopped, for garnish

Preheat oven to 400°.

To prepare the lobster stock, roast the lobster and shrimp shells in the oven until they are well caramelized.

Place the roasted shells and all the remaining stock ingredients in a large pot and bring them to a simmer. Simmer gently for 30 minutes. Skim the foam from the surface of the stock and pass the remainder through a fine-mesh strainer and into a bowl. Set aside.

To prepare the bisque, wipe the stock pot clean and return it to the stove. Over medium heat, melt all but 1 tablespoon of the butter. Add the shallots and garlic and sauté, stirring with a wooden spoon, until the vegetables are translucent. Add the tomatoes and cook for 10 minutes, stirring occasionally.

Add the wine and reduce the mixture by ⅔. Add the cream and previously prepared lobster stock and simmer for 10 minutes.

Place the flour in a small bowl and mix the remaining butter into it. Add this roux to the soup and stir well and simmer 5 minutes more, until the bisque thickens slightly.

Add the lemon juice and bring the bisque back to a simmer. Strain it through a fine-mesh strainer and adjust the seasoning, if necessary, with salt and red pepper flakes.

To serve, place the lobster meat in individual bowls and ladle the bisque on top. Garnish each bowl with a light drizzle of Meyer lemon olive oil and chopped chives or tarragon.

DELORIMIER WINERY

It's well-known at deLorimier that our tasting room manager/chef, Ryan Waldron, loves bacon. He firmly holds the belief that bacon makes everything – well, almost everything – taste better. He proves his point with this recipe, in which crispy bacon and its drippings add a luxurious dimension to beef stew.

2001 Highway 128 | Geyserville, CA 95441
707-857-2000
delorimierwinery.com

RYAN'S ROMANTIC
ROSEMARY & BACON BEEF STEW

Pair with deLorimier Crazy Creek Vineyard Cabernet Sauvignon

SERVES 6-8

6 ounces thick-cut bacon

3 tablespoons flour

1 teaspoon salt

½ teaspoon freshly ground
pepper

3 pounds boneless beef chuck,
cut into chunks

½ pound baby carrots

½ pound pearl onions

3 garlic cloves, minced

1 cup dry red wine

1 cup beef broth

3 tablespoons tomato paste

1 tablespoon fresh rosemary,
minced

In a large frying pan, cook the bacon strips until they're crispy. Transfer them to paper towels to drain, reserving the drippings in the pan. When the bacon has cooled, chop the strips into small pieces.

In a large bowl, combine the flour, salt and pepper and mix well. Add the beef chunks to the flour mixture and toss to coat them evenly.

Pour out and reserve ½ of the bacon drippings in the pan and heat the remaining ½ over medium-high heat. When the drippings are hot, add ½ of the floured beef chunks and cook, turning once, until they're well-browned, about 5 minutes on each side. Transfer the beef to a slow cooker.

Add the reserved drippings back to the pan and brown the rest of the meat. Add the carrots, onions and garlic halfway through browning the second batch. When the meat is browned, transfer it and the vegetables to the slow cooker.

Return the frying pan to medium-high heat and add the wine, broth and tomato paste. Stir well, then bring the mixture to a boil and deglaze the pan, stirring to scrape up the browned bits on the bottom. Pour the contents of the pan over the vegetables and beef.

Cover the slow cooker and cook the stew on the high-heat setting for 4-5 hours, or the low-heat setting for 8-9 hours. Add the chopped bacon and fresh rosemary. Raise the heat for 10 minutes to thicken the stew. Season with salt and pepper to taste, and ladle into warmed bowls.

DUTCHER CROSSING WINERY

Dutcher Crossing owner Debra Mathy and Wine Road Northern Sonoma County have a prophetic connection: It was during Winter WineLAND in January 2007 that Debra made her successful offer to purchase the Dry Creek Valley winery. This rich, velvety butternut squash bisque is a great fall-winter warmer, and its cream base is complemented by our Stuhlmuller Chardonnay.

8533 Dry Creek Road | Healdsburg, CA 95448
707-431-2700
dutchercrossingwinery.com

VEGI

BUTTERNUT SQUASH
BISQUE

Pair with Dutcher Crossing Stuhlmuller Vineyard Alexander Valley Chardonnay

SERVES 10-12

5 pounds butternut squash

4 tablespoons olive oil plus more for rubbing

1 large yellow onion, diced

vegetable stock

salt and pepper, to taste

3 cups heavy cream

Preheat oven to 350°.

Cut the squash(es) in ½ lengthwise and remove the seeds. Lightly rub the squash flesh with olive oil; you don't need to peel the squash.

Place the squash halves on a cookie sheet and roast them in the oven until they are fork-tender; cooking time will depend on the size of the pieces, so check at 30 minutes or so for doneness.

Remove the roasted squash from the oven and allow the pieces to cool until they can be comfortably handled. Scoop out the flesh and set it aside, discarding the shell.

In a sauté pan, cook the onion in the olive oil until it's golden. Add the squash to the pan, and then add enough vegetable stock to just cover the squash. Simmer over medium heat for 30-45 minutes.

Remove the pan from the stove and transfer the mixture to a pot. Using an immersion blender, puree the squash until it's smooth. Return the bisque to the stove and warm it over medium heat. Add salt and pepper to taste, and finish with heavy cream to your desired consistency. Heat the bisque through and serve warm.

MALM CELLARS

The winery is so close to the diVine restaurant that I have had many opportunities to enjoy Michael Kennedy's potato bacon soup ... too many, perhaps! It's a great match with our Chardonnay.

119 W. North Street | Healdsburg CA 95448
707-364-0441
malmcellars.com

POTATO BACON SOUP

Pair with Malm Cellars Chardonnay

SERVES 15

⅛ cup olive oil

2 tablespoons butter

½ cup white onions,
   finely chopped

½ cup carrots, finely chopped

¾ tablespoon garlic, chopped

3 pounds russet potatoes,
   peeled and cubed

1 pound bacon, chopped

4 tablespoons roasted garlic

2 tablespoons chipotle pesto

2 tablespoons chicken base

½ tablespoon black pepper

½ cup salt

½ gallon heavy cream

4 ounces cornstarch

In a large pot, add the olive oil and butter, and melt them together over medium heat. Add the onions, carrots and garlic, and simmer the mixture for 10 minutes, or until the vegetables are soft.

Fill the pot halfway with water and add the potatoes, bacon, roasted garlic, chipotle pesto, chicken base, pepper and salt. Mix all the ingredients and bring them to a boil. Reduce the heat to a simmer and cook for 30 minutes, stirring occasionally.

Stir in the cream. In a small bowl, dissolve the cornstarch in warm water and slowly add it to the pot, to thicken the soup. Serve warm.

PARADISE RIDGE WINERY

I have created recipes for Paradise Ridge for about four years now and am passionate about wine and food pairing. One of my favorite projects at the winery was to create a pairing program that showcased the broad attributes wine has with herbs used in cooking. This vegan recipe pairs nicely with big red wines and doesn't skimp on flavor.

4545 Thomas Lake Harris Drive | Santa Rosa, CA 95403
707-528-9463
prwinery.com

VEGI

CARROT POTATO BISQUE
WITH ROASTED PEPPER & CILANTRO

Pair with Paradise Ridge The Posse Red Blend

SERVES 8

STOCK

1 sweet potato, chopped
2 shallots, chopped
3 yellow onions, coarsely chopped
1 pound crimini mushrooms, sliced
4 cloves garlic, crushed
4 carrots with green tops, chopped
2 parsnips, peeled and chopped
1 rutabaga, peeled and chopped
1 apple, cored and quartered
1 leek, greens chopped
   (reserve white for bisque)
1 teaspoon ground cumin
1 teaspoon salt
½ teaspoon pepper
2 12-ounce bottles Guinness draught beer
1 bottle blanc de blancs sparkling wine

BISQUE

1 tablespoon olive oil
5 carrots, peeled and chopped
1 yellow onion, chopped
4 potatoes, peeled and chopped
4 roasted red bell peppers (skins
   removed) and chopped
white part of 1 leek
1 teaspoon ground cumin
1 teaspoon salt
½ teaspoon fresh-ground black pepper
2-4 cups root vegetable stock
1 cup cilantro, chopped, plus 2
   tablespoons for garnish
1 cup crème fraiche

Preheat oven to 350°.

Place all the stock ingredients except for the sparkling wine in a 9-inch by 11-inch baking dish. Bake for 30 minutes, then check the fluid (watch closely, as you don't want the vegetables to burn). When most of the fluid has been reduced and browning has started, add the sparkling wine to rehydrate the vegetables. Continue to bake the mixture for an additional 20 minutes, or until the liquid has been reduced by ⅓.

Put the mixture through a fine-mesh sieve, retaining the stock and discarding the solids.

To prepare the bisque, add the olive oil to a large stock pot set over medium-high heat. Add the carrots and onions and cook until the onions turn opaque. Add the potatoes, roasted peppers, leek whites, salt, cumin and black pepper and stir to combine. Add approximately 2-3 cups of the root vegetable stock and cook for 1 hour, or until the vegetables are tender. If necessary, add more stock to keep the mixture moist. Add the cilantro in the final 5 minutes of cooking and stir to blend.

Serve the bisque in individual bowls, each topped with a dollop of crème fraiche and a sprinkling of chopped cilantro.

PEZZI KING

Be sure to start this hearty, flavor-packed stew well in advance, as the beans need to soak overnight or for at least 8 hours. The ingredients list is long, but the preparation is easy and the results deliciously rewarding! As a shortcut, use your favorite tomatillo salsa, though freshly made is always best.

412 Hudson Street | Healdsburg, CA 95448
866-473-4309
pezziking.com

PORK & BLACK BEAN STEW
WITH ROASTED RED PEPPER & TOMATILLO SALSA

Pair with Pezzi King Oakey Grande Zinfandel

SERVES 6

STEW

1 pound dried black beans
1 tablespoon chili powder
2 teaspoons cumin seeds, toasted and crushed
¼ teaspoon cayenne pepper
1 teaspoon dried basil
½ teaspoon freshly ground black pepper
1 teaspoon kosher salt
2 pounds cubed pork stew meat
    (from shoulder or roast)
4 ounces pancetta or bacon, chopped
1-½ tablespoons vegetable oil
3 cloves garlic, chopped
1 medium yellow onion, chopped
2 stalks celery, ends trimmed and diced
1 large red bell pepper, cored, seeded
    and chopped
2 jalapeno chiles, seeded and minced
2 tablespoons fresh oregano, chopped,
    or 1 tablespoon dried
1 cup red wine
2-½ cups chicken stock
½ cup cilantro, chopped
1 bay leaf
10 whole cloves

SALSA

1 tablespoon vegetable oil
1 pound tomatillos, husks removed, washed
    and chopped
1 medium yellow onion, sliced
1 shallot, chopped
1 clove garlic, chopped
1 jalapeno chile, minced (include seeds for
    more heat)
1 roasted red bell pepper, seeded and chopped
½ teaspoon cumin seeds, toasted
⅓ cup cilantro, chopped
kosher salt, to taste
black pepper, to taste
sour cream, for garnish

Soak the beans in cold water for 8 hours or overnight. Strain them and rinse with water.

In a large bowl, mix together the chili powder, cumin, cayenne, basil, black pepper and salt. Add the pork to the bowl and mixing thoroughly to coat the meat with the seasonings.

In a large heavy-bottomed stock pot, cook the pancetta (or bacon) over medium heat until the pieces are very lightly browned. Using a slotted spoon, transfer the pancetta to paper towels.

Add the vegetable oil to the same pot and increase the heat to medium-high. Add the seasoned pork, garlic, onion, celery, red pepper, jalapenos and oregano and sauté for 10 minutes, until the meat is lightly browned. Add the pancetta, red wine, chicken stock, beans, cilantro, bay leaf and cloves and bring the mixture to a boil. Reduce the heat to a simmer, cover the pot, and cook for 1 hour.

While the stew cooks, prepare the salsa. In a large sauté pan, heat the oil over medium heat. Add the tomatillos, onion, shallot, garlic, jalapenos, roasted red pepper and cumin seed and sauté, stirring often, for 10-12 minutes, until the tomatillos begin to soften and the onions turn translucent. Remove the mixture from the heat and allow it to cool. Add the cilantro, season with salt and pepper, and mix thoroughly.

To serve the stew, place the pork and black beans in a large bowl and top them with tomatillo salsa and a small dollop of sour cream.

RIDGE VINEYARDS

LYTTON SPRINGS

Smoky lentils and bacon make this soup
a natural pairing for Ridge Zinfandel. Its
simplicity really showcases what wine country
is all about, with locally sourced ingredients
and, of course, the symbiotic nature of food
and wine when they're enjoyed together.

650 Lytton Springs Road | Healdsburg, CA 95448
707-433-7721
ridgewine.com

WINE COUNTRY

SMOKED BACON & LENTIL SOUP

Pair with Ridge Lytton Springs Zinfandel

SERVES 6

2 tablespoons olive oil

4 quarts white onions, diced

2 quarts celery, diced

2 quarts carrots, diced

10 cloves garlic, minced

½ pound smoked bacon, chopped

2 bunches parsley, chopped and divided

2 bunches thyme, chopped and divided

2 bunches basil, chopped and divided

4 quarts black lentils

6 quarts vegetable or chicken stock

In a stock pot, heat the olive oil over medium-high heat. Add the onions, celery, carrots, garlic, bacon and ½ of the herbs, and cook until the vegetables are translucent and the fat has rendered from the bacon.

Add the lentils and stir briskly. Add the stock, making sure the liquid covers the lentils by at least 2 inches. Bring the mixture to a simmer and cook until the lentils are tender, about 1 hour.

When the lentils are done, add the remaining fresh herbs and season the soup with salt and pepper to taste.

ROBERT RUE VINEYARD

This soup is like the basic black dress or a black suit in your closet. It's a reliable standby, always in fashion. Top it with sour cream or salsa to add both eye appeal and additional flavor.

1406 Wood Road | Fulton, CA 95439
707-578-1601
robertruevineyard.com

VEGI

BLACK BEAN SOUP

Pair with Robert Rue Zinfandel

SERVES 8-10

2 tablespoons olive oil

6 cloves garlic, minced

4 carrots, chopped

4 celery stalks, chopped

2 onions, chopped

3 teaspoons chili powder

4 teaspoons ground cumin

4 cups vegetable broth

1 cup Robert Rue Zinfandel

6 15-ounce cans black beans

3 cups frozen corn

2 15-ounce cans tomato sauce

½ teaspoon black pepper

cilantro, chopped, for garnish

In a large saucepan, heat the oil over medium heat. Add the garlic, carrots, celery and onions and sauté, stirring occasionally, until the onions are soft.

Add the chili powder and cumin to the pan and cook for 1 minute, stirring. Add the vegetable broth, wine, 3 of the cans of beans, corn, 1 can of tomato sauce and the black pepper. Bring the mixture to a boil.

In a food processor, puree the remaining 3 cans of beans and 1 can of tomato sauce. Add the puree to the pot and stir to combine. Reduce the heat, cover the pot, and simmer the soup until the carrots are tender. Enjoy!

SANGLIER CELLARS

Beans and cornbread were family staples for my husband, winemaker Glenn Alexander, when he grew up in rural East Texas. Heirloom Rancho Gordo beans, and abundant fresh herbs from our garden, transform this simple farmer's meal into a comforting and flavorful dish that complements our Pinot Noir.

132 Plaza Street | Healdsburg, CA 95448
707-433-6104
sangliercellars.com

BLACK CALYPSO BEAN SOUP
WITH HAM BONE

Pair with Sanglier Russian River Valley Pinot Noir

SERVES 8

2 cups dried Rancho Gordo Black Calypso beans

2 thyme sprigs

2 flat leaf parsley sprigs

1 bay leaf

2 tablespoons extra virgin olive oil, plus more for drizzling

1 onion, chopped

1 stalk celery, chopped

2 carrots, chopped

1 large ham bone with scraps of meat attached

3 cups chicken broth

salt and freshly ground pepper

Parmigiano-Reggiano, grated, for garnish

wine vinegar, for garnish

Place the beans in a pot with enough water to cover them by 2 inches and let them soak overnight. You can also parboil and soak them for 1 hour. Rinse the soaked beans and reserve them.

Put the thyme sprigs, parsley and bay leaf on a square of cheesecloth and tie the bundle securely with cooking twine.

In a soup pot over medium heat, warm the olive oil. Add the onion, celery and carrot. Sauté until the vegetables begin to soften and caramelize, about 10 minutes. Add the drained beans, cheesecloth bundle, ham bone, chicken broth and enough cold water to cover the contents by about 1 inch. Lower the heat and cook for 2-3 hours, allowing the steam to vent.

Cook the beans until they are meltingly soft. Remove the ham bone and cheesecloth bundle. Cut off and reserve any bits of meat still clinging to the ham bone. Season the beans with salt and pepper to taste. Stir in the reserved bits of meat from the bone.

Ladle the soup into serving bowls. Sprinkle Parmigiano-Reggiano on top of the soup, and add a drizzle of olive oil and a drop of wine vinegar to each bowl. Serve with warm cornbread.

SIMONCINI VINEYARDS

This meatball soup recipe comes from Anna, Val Peline's mother, and from the Italian village of Santo Stefano in the Abruzzo region, Province of L'Aquila. We thank Val for sharing his family recipes with us. It warms the heart as well as the stomach!

2303 West Dry Creek Road | Healdsburg, CA 95448
707-433-8811
simoncinivineyards.com

STRACCIATELLE

Pair with Simoncini Estate Zinfandel Rosé

SERVES 10

72 ounces chicken stock (Swanson 99% fat free)

3 carrots, peeled and julienned

1-½ cups parsley, chopped and divided

½ pound spinach, blanched and roughly chopped

½ pound ground round beef (80%)

½ pound ground pork

1 cup Italian bread crumbs

1 cup Parmesan cheese, grated, plus more to finish

1 large yellow onion, finely chopped

6 large eggs

½ cup orzo pasta

salt and black pepper, to taste

To prepare the broth, add the chicken stock to a large soup pot, along with the carrots, ¾ cup of the parsley, spinach and 15 grinds of black pepper. Bring the mixture to a boil, then lower to a simmer for 15 minutes.

While the broth is simmering, prepare the meatballs. Combine the beef, pork, bread crumbs, Parmesan, remaining ¾ cup parsley, onion and 2 of the eggs in a large bowl. Season with salt and pepper, and mix well.

Drop approximately 130 free-formed meatballs, each the size of a dime, into the simmering broth and continue the low boil for 15 minutes. Free-forming the meatballs allows some of the parsley and onion to release into the soup, adding flavor.

Add the orzo and continue the low boil for 9 minutes.

Crack the remaining 4 eggs into a bowl. Pierce the yolks with a fork and stir to break them up, keeping as much of the yolks and whites separate as you can – do not scramble. Drizzle the egg mixture into the simmering broth while slowly stirring.

Season with more salt and pepper, if necessary, and top the soup with additional grated Parmesan.

TAFT STREET WINERY

Crab season on the North Coast begins in early November, and every year we look forward to our favorite ways of feasting on the local Dungeness variety. While we usually just crack them and have them with a baguette, butter, salad and Taft Street Chardonnay, here is another great way to enjoy the world's best crab.

2030 Barlow Lane | Sebastopol, CA 95472
707-823-2049
taftstreetwinery.com

CHEF MIKE TIERNEY

TAFT STREET
CRAB CHOWDER

Pair with Taft Street Russian River Valley Chardonnay

SERVES 10

6 slices bacon

1 tablespoon butter

1 yellow onion, chopped

1 green bell pepper, chopped

½ cup celery, diced

2 garlic cloves, minced

½ cup Taft Street Chardonnay

1 tablespoon fresh basil, chopped

1 teaspoon fresh black pepper

1 teaspoon dried thyme

2 teaspoons Worcestershire sauce

4 potatoes, peeled and diced

1-½ quarts chicken stock

½ cup butter

½ cup flour

1 quart half and half

1 teaspoon saffron threads

lumpmeat from 3 fresh crabs

chopped parsley, for garnish

In a sauté pan, brown the bacon and allow it to cool. Crumble the strips and set them aside with the bacon grease.

In the same pan, melt the butter and add the onion, green pepper, celery and garlic, and cook for 10 minutes. Add the Chardonnay and bring the mixture to a simmer. Add the basil, black pepper, thyme and Worcestershire sauce. Add the potatoes and chicken stock, bring the mixture to a boil, and simmer for 10 minutes.

While the soup simmers, melt the butter in a small skillet over low heat. Add the flour to make a roux, stirring for about 10 minutes.

Stir the roux into the soup, and add the half and half, reserved bacon and ½ of its grease. Cook until the potatoes are tender and the soup has thickened, about 15 minutes. Stir in the saffron threads and crab. When the soup is heated through, serve it with parsley as a garnish.

PASTA & RICE

Applewood Bacon Macaroni & Cheese

Pancetta Mac 'n Cheese

Penne with Pumpkin & Smoked Turkey

Ragu d'Agnello con Orecchiette

Farro Salad with Butternut Squash

Ravioli Bertapelle

Wild Boar Ragu with Crimini Mushrooms & Dried Cherries over Polenta

Cabernet Cavatelli with Duck & Mushroom Ragu

Lobster & Saffron Ravioli with Brown Butter & Sage

Nonna's Puttanesca Sauce

CLOS DU BOIS WINERY

What's better than macaroni and cheese? Mac and cheese with applewood bacon! The intense, aromatic meatiness of smoked bacon complements the bold, rich flavors of our Bordeaux-style Marlstone red blend.

19410 Geyserville Avenue | Geyserville, CA 95441
800-222-3189
closdubois.com

APPLEWOOD BACON
MACARONI & CHEESE

Pair with Marlstone Alexander Valley

SERVES 6 AS A SIDE

10 cups water

kosher salt

3 cups elbow macaroni

½ pound applewood-smoked bacon

1 quart heavy cream

2 cloves garlic, peeled and lightly crushed

2 tablespoons Dijon mustard

3-½ cups Gruyere cheese, grated

freshly ground white pepper

½ cup Parmesan cheese, finely grated

½ cup sharp Cheddar cheese, finely grated

Worcestershire sauce, to taste

bottled hot sauce, to taste

½ cup toasted bread crumbs or panko bread crumbs

Preheat oven to 350°.

In a large pot, bring the water to a rolling boil. Add salt and taste the water; it should be salty like sea water. Add the macaroni and stir with a wooden spoon to ensure the macaroni does not stick to the bottom of the pot as it cooks. Cook until the macaroni is still quite firm, 8-10 minutes.

In a large skillet, cook the bacon over medium heat until the strips are crisp, and transfer them to paper towels to drain.

Pour the macaroni and water into a strainer placed over the sink. Allow the water to drain out, reserving approximately 1 cup of the liquid.

In the same pot, bring the cream, garlic and reserved cooking liquid to a simmer. Add the mustard and 3 cups of the Gruyere. Season with salt and white pepper to taste. Simmer the mixture gently, stirring constantly, until the cheese is melted and has integrated with the cream. Add the Parmesan and Cheddar. Stir and simmer the cheese sauce until it's smooth. Add a splash each of Worcestershire and hot sauce, and stir to blend. Taste for seasoning.

Add the macaroni to the cheese sauce and stir gently. Allow the macaroni to rest on the stove, off the heat, for 5-10 minutes, so the pasta absorbs the flavors. Remove and discard the garlic.

Place the bread crumbs in a small bowl, crumble in the bacon and combine the ingredients. Fill a baking dish with the macaroni mixture. Top it with the bread crumb/bacon mixture and the remaining Gruyere, and bake 10-12 minutes or until the bread crumbs form a crusty top. Serve immediately.

COLAGROSSI WINERY

America's beloved mac and cheese has its roots in Italy, where macaroni pasta originated. Chef Jennifer McMurry gives the dish even more *gusto di Italia* by adding pancetta, the Italian version of bacon. Pancetta is pork belly that has been cured – not smoked like bacon – and infused with dried herbs, black pepper and other spices. It adds a distinctive zing to the dish and its porky flavor ties nicely with Pinot Noir.

3360 Coffey Lane, Suite E | Santa Rosa, 95403
707-529-5459
colagrossiwines.com

PANCETTA
MAC 'N CHEESE

Pair with Colagrossi Russian River Valley Pinot Noir

SERVES 4-5

¾ ounce butter

2 tablespoons flour

2 cups milk

¼ teaspoon salt

pinch white pepper

pinch freshly grated nutmeg

1-pound package dried macaroni

½ cup pancetta, chopped

1-½ cup toasted bread crumbs

1 cup Monterey Jack cheese, grated

1 cup Estero Gold cheese, grated

Prepare a béchamel sauce by melting the butter in a skillet. Stir in the flour. Slowly add the milk, whisking as you go; add only a small amount of milk at a time, making sure that it is completely incorporated before adding more. Cook the sauce over low to medium heat, stirring constantly, until it comes to a boil. Add the salt, pepper and nutmeg, stir, and remove from the heat.

Cook the macaroni according to package directions. While the pasta cooks, place the pancetta in a sauté pan over medium heat and cook until the pieces are crispy and the fat rendered. Add the bread crumbs to the pan and blend with the pancetta.

Add the cooked pasta to the skillet with the warm béchamel. Add both cheeses and mix together. Place the pasta in a serving dish and crumble the bread crumb/pancetta mixture over the top. Serve immediately.

DELOACH VINEYARDS

This is a comforting dish that makes great use of leftover Thanksgiving turkey. For an elegant presentation, serve the pasta in small, hollowed-out sugar pumpkins. Stuff the pumpkins ahead and bake them in the oven for 30 minutes. Then garnish with more cheese.

1791 Olivet Road | Santa Rosa, CA 95401
707-526-9111
deloachvineyards.com

PENNE
WITH PUMPKIN & SMOKED TURKEY

Pair with DeLoach Russian River Valley Chardonnay

SERVES 4

1 pound penne rigate

1 tablespoon extra virgin olive oil

4 cloves garlic, finely chopped

1 medium onion, finely chopped

1 bay leaf, fresh or dried

4-6 sprigs sage leaves, cut into chiffonade

1 cup dry white wine

1 cup chicken stock

1 cup canned pumpkin

1 cup heavy cream

⅛ teaspoon ground cinnamon

⅛ teaspoon ground nutmeg

coarse salt and black pepper

1 cup smoked turkey, diced

several handfuls of spinach or chard, cut into chiffonade

1 cup Parmesan or Romano cheese, grated

Cook the penne pasta al dente, according to package directions. Drain the pasta in a colander.

Heat a large nonstick skillet over medium-high heat. Add the olive oil to the pan, swirl, and then add the garlic and onion. Sauté 3-5 minutes, until the onions are tender.

Add the bay leaf, sage and wine to the pan. Reduce the wine by ½, about 2 minutes. Add the chicken stock and pumpkin to the skillet, stir to combine, and cook the sauce, stirring constantly, until it bubbles. Lower the heat and stir in the cream, cinnamon, nutmeg, salt and pepper. Simmer the mixture 5-10 minutes to thicken the sauce, adding the turkey in the last 2 minutes.

Return the drained pasta to the pot in which it was cooked. Remove the bay leaf from the pumpkin turkey sauce and pour it over the pasta. Toss the pasta and sauce and cook over low heat for 1 minute. Add the greens and allow them to wilt just a bit. Add the cheese, remove the pot from the heat, and toss 1 more time before serving.

HKG ESTATE WINERY/HOP KILN VINEYARDS

Originating from the southern Italian region of Puglia, orecchiette pasta resembles little ears (orecchio means ear in Italian). When cooked al dente (firm), orecchiette are sturdy enough to trap sauce – in this case, Chef Renzo's lamb sauce infused with HKG Pinot Noir and slow-cooked for hours. It's *delizioso!*

6050 Westside Road | Healdsburg, CA 95448
707-433-6491
hkgwines.com

RAGU D'AGNELLO
CON ORECCHIETTE

Pair with HKG Estate Russian River Valley Pinot Noir

SERVES 6

¼ cup extra virgin olive oil

1 large white onion, coarsely chopped

5 celery ribs, coarsely chopped

3 carrots, coarsely chopped

2 pounds ground lamb

1 cup HKG Pinot Noir

3 14.5-ounce cans tomato sauce

3 cups beef broth

1 tablespoon tarragon, chopped

1 tablespoon rosemary, chopped

1 cup kalamata olives, pitted and quartered

1 cup roasted red bell pepper, diced

1 box dried orechielte pasta

salt and pepper

Heat the olive oil in a medium-sized pot. Add the onions, celery and carrots and sauté until the vegetables are softened.

Add the lamb and cook, stirring, until the meat is slightly cooked. Add the wine, tomato sauce and beef broth. Add the tarragon and rosemary, and cook on low heat for 2-½ hours, stirring occasionally. Occasionally skim the fat from the surface as the sauce cooks.

In the 20 minutes before the sauce is done, cook the orechiette per the instructions on the box. Drain well.

When the sauce is cooked through, stir in the olives and roasted pepper, and let the sauce stand for 10 minutes to allow the flavors to infuse. Season with salt and pepper to taste.

Add the sauce to the cooked pasta, toss and serve.

HOOK & LADDER

VINEYARDS AND WINERY

Christine De Loach created this dish for her aunt's 95th birthday luncheon, an outdoor, all-afternoon event. There are several vegetarians in the family – the family doctor was also in attendance – so the side salad had to be nutritious and served without being refrigerated, yet with plenty of flavor. This dish is wonderful for a large crowd, and much of it can be prepared in advance. Farro, a small grain in the wheat family, can be cooked, drained and frozen for up to one month. Butternut squash can be roasted, peeled and cubed the day before the salad is completed.

2134 Olivet Road | Santa Rosa, CA 95401
707-526-2255
hookandladderwinery.com

VEGI

FARRO SALAD
WITH BUTTERNUT SQUASH

Pair with Hook & Ladder Station Ten

SERVES 12

1 medium butternut squash

1 tablespoon butter

3 cups pearled farro

⅓ cup dried cranberries

½ cup pine nuts

1 medium red onion, finely diced

1 red bell pepper, finely diced

2 garlic cloves, minced

1 large tomato, finely diced

1 cup arugula, stems removed

¼ cup red wine vinegar

½ cup Hook & Ladder extra
   virgin olive oil

1-½ tablespoons kosher salt

1 tablespoon freshly ground
   black pepper

Preheat oven to 350°.

Split the butternut squash lengthwise and remove the seeds. Rub butter on the cut side of the squash halves, season them with salt and pepper, and roast for 45 minutes, or until they're tender. Peel and cut the squash into ½-inch cubes and set aside.

In a large pot, bring 7 cups of salted water to a boil. Add the farro and reduce the heat. Simmer the grains until they're tender, 15-20 minutes. DO NOT overcook. Drain the farro in a colander, then spread the grains on a sheet pan and allow them to cool slightly and dry.

While the farro cooks and cools, soak the dried cranberries in hot water until they're softened, approximately 30 minutes, and allow them to drain. Over medium heat, toast the pine nuts in a small skillet.

In a large bowl, combine the cooked squash, farro, hydrated cranberries, pine nuts, onion, bell pepper, garlic, tomato and arugula. In a small bowl, combine the vinegar, olive oil, salt and pepper and add the dressing to the salad. Taste for seasonings and adjust if needed. Serve at room temperature.

HUDSON STREET WINERIES

My mother taught me to make ravioli with hand-rolled pasta and handmade pillows. It became a New Year's tradition in our home, where I would spend four football games making ravioli, only to see the meal devoured in one halftime. I've been tweaking this sauce for 30 years. *Mangia bene!*

428 Hudson Street | Healdsburg, CA 95448
707-433-2364
hudsonstreetwineries.com

RAVIOLI
BERTAPELLE

Pair with Bertapelle Cellars Russian River Valley Petite Sirah

SERVES 10-12

1 ounce dried porcini mushrooms

2 tablespoons olive oil

½ pound lean ground beef

¼ pound spicy ground sausage

1 cup Bertapelle Petite Sirah, divided

¼ pound fresh crimini mushrooms, chopped

1 teaspoon dried rosemary

1 teaspoon dried thyme

2 teaspoons oregano

½ large onion, chopped

2 cloves garlic, finely chopped

¼ bunch Italian parsley leaves, chopped

1 stalk celery, chopped

1 large carrot, chopped

1 15-ounce can tomato sauce

1 6-ounce can tomato paste

1 28-ounce can Italian-style tomatoes, diced

1 teaspoon sugar

1 teaspoon salt

1 teaspoon freshly ground black pepper

72-80 ravioli pillows

Parmesan cheese, grated

Soak the dried porcini mushrooms in 1 cup of warm water for 30 minutes. Drain and rough-chop the mushrooms, reserving the water. Strain the mushroom water through a coffee filter and set it and the mushrooms aside.

In a large skillet, heat the olive oil and brown the ground beef and sausage. Drain the fat from the skillet. Add ¼ cup of the wine and simmer the mixture until no liquid remains.

In a large pot, add the beef/sausage mixture, reserved mushroom water and remaining wine. Add the rehydrated and fresh mushrooms and all remaining ingredients except the ravioli pillows and Parmesan. Bring the mixture to a boil, reduce the heat and simmer 1-2 hours.

Before you are ready to serve the dish, bring a large pot of water, 1 tablespoon of olive oil and 1 teaspoon of salt to a full boil. Add the ravioli pillows. Bring the water back to a boil and cook the ravioli another 4 minutes. Drain them and place 6-8 ravioli pillows in individual pasta bowls, and cover with the sauce. Top with Parmesan cheese.

KOKOMO WINERY

Wild boar is relatively easy to find from Sonoma County butchers and some gourmet markets. If you can't find boar, use lamb, venison or pork shoulder instead.

4791 Dry Creek Road | Healdsburg, CA 95448
707-433-0200
kokomowines.com

WILD BOAR RAGU

WITH CRIMINI MUSHROOMS & DRIED CHERRIES OVER POLENTA

Pair with Kokomo Pinot Noir

SERVES 6

RAGU

4 tablespoons olive oil

¼ pound pancetta or bacon, cut into small dice

1-½ pounds wild boar shoulder, cut into ½-inch cubes

1 cup yellow onions, finely chopped

½ cup celery, finely chopped

½ cup carrots, finely chopped

1 pound crimini mushrooms, stems removed and sliced

1 tablespoon garlic, minced

1 cup Kokomo Pinot Noir

1 14-ounce can diced tomatoes and juice

1 cup pork or chicken stock

1 tablespoon salt

½ teaspoon cracked black pepper

1 tablespoon fresh sage leaves, chopped

1 tablespoon fresh thyme leaves, chopped

½ cup dried Bing cherries

minced parsley, for garnish

POLENTA

3 cups water

3 cups milk

2 teaspoons salt

1-½ cups yellow cornmeal

3 tablespoons unsalted butter

½ cup Pecorino Romano cheese

To prepare the ragu, heat the oil in a large, heavy pot over medium-high heat. Add the pancetta or bacon and sauté, stirring often, until the fat is rendered and the pancetta is light brown and crisp, about 2 minutes. Season the boar with salt and pepper, and add the meat to the pan. Cook until it's browned on all sides, 7-10 minutes. Add the onions, celery, carrots and mushrooms and cook, stirring often, until the mixture is very soft and starting to caramelize, 10-12 minutes. Add the garlic and cook for 1 minute.

Deglaze the pan with the wine and cook until the liquid is nearly evaporated, 3-4 minutes. Add the tomatoes and their juices, stock, salt, pepper, sage, thyme and cherries, and bring to a boil. Reduce the heat to medium-low, cover the pan, and simmer the ragu, stirring occasionally, until the meat is very tender and the sauce is thick and fragrant, about 1-½ hours.

To prepare the polenta, bring the water and milk to a boil in a large, heavy saucepan. Add the salt. Gradually whisk in the cornmeal. Reduce the heat to low and cook until the mixture thickens and the cornmeal is tender, stirring often, about 15 minutes. Turn off the heat. Add the butter and cheese, and stir until they're melted.

Serve the ragu over the polenta, and garnish with the minced parsley.

SIMI WINERY

This recipe takes a little time but is worth it in the end! It's a rich and hearty pasta dish that will be most welcome on a cool, crisp harvest night. Cavatelli are small gnocchi that are popular throughout Italy.

16275 Healdsburg Avenue | Healdsburg, CA 95448
707-433-6981
simiwinery.com

CABERNET CAVATELLI
WITH DUCK & MUSHROOM RAGU

Pair with Simi Reserve Cabernet Sauvignon

SERVES 6
RAGU

1-½ pounds boneless duck leg meat, cut into chunks

1 tablespoon mild paprika

salt and pepper

2 tablespoons olive oil

¼ cup shiitake mushrooms, stemmed and sliced thin

¼ cup button mushrooms, sliced thin

¼ cup oyster mushrooms, stemmed and sliced thin

¼ large onion, small dice

1 carrot, small dice

1 celery stalk, small dice

1 clove garlic, minced

1 cup canned crushed San Marzano tomatoes

1 cup Cabernet Sauvignon

8 black peppercorns

8 parsley sprigs

2 rosemary sprigs

1 bay leaf

3-4 cups duck or chicken stock

CAVATELLI

7 ounces 00 or all-purpose flour

1 ounce Cabernet grape skin flour

5 ounces fresh ricotta cheese

2 large eggs

3-4 tablespoons Grana Padano cheese, grated

3-4 tablespoons unsalted butter

To prepare the ragu, place the duck in a bowl and add the paprika, salt and pepper. Stir the duck pieces to coat them evenly with the seasonings.

Heat the oil in a heavy-bottomed pot and sear the duck until the pieces are golden brown. Remove them and set aside. Add to the pot the mushrooms, onions, carrot and celery. Cook until the onions are translucent. Add the cooked meat and garlic. Cook for 1 minute. Add the tomatoes and break them up with a spoon. Cook for 4 minutes. Pour in the wine, scraping the pan as you stir. Simmer until the mixture is reduced by ½.

Preheat oven to 325°.

Put the peppercorns, parsley, rosemary and bay leaf on a square of cheesecloth and fold it around the herbs to make a pouch, tying it closed with cooking twine. Add the pouch and enough stock to almost cover the meat. Return the mixture to a simmer, cover the pot, and place it in the preheated oven. Cook for approximately 2 hours, until the duck falls apart and the sauce is thick. Season with salt and pepper.

To make the cavatelli, mix the 2 flours, ricotta and eggs in a large bowl and knead the dough with your hands for about 5 minutes. Using a cavatelli maker, roll out the dough ¼-inch thick and cut it into strips. Run each strip through the cavatelli cutter.

Bring a large pot of salted water to a boil. Add the cavatelli and cook them for 5-6 minutes, until they're tender yet firm. Drain the pasta and add it to the ragu, along with the Grana Padano and butter. Mix until the pasta absorbs the sauce and becomes creamy. Season and serve.

THUMBPRINT CELLARS

Winemaker/owner Scott Lindstrom-Dake has been asked to make another Chardonnay since his amazing 2005 release. Well, he listened. Scott crafted two distinct styles of Chardonnay from the 2012 vintage, so we decided to showcase his barrel-aged Russian River Valley version with ... wait for it ... lobster ravioli! The richness of Ryan Tunheim's creation makes this a deliciously decadent companion for our new Chardonnay.

102 Matheson Street | Healdsburg, CA 95448
707-433-2393
thumbprintcellars.com

LOBSTER & SAFFRON RAVIOLI
WITH BROWN BUTTER & SAGE

Pair with Thumbprint Cellars Catie's Corner Russian River Valley Chardonnay

SERVES 4

RAVIOLI FILLING

2 ounces unsalted butter

1 clove garlic, chopped

1 tablespoon shallots, chopped

16 ounces lobster meat

1 tablespoon chives, chopped

2 ounces Thumbprint Cellars Chardonnay

2 ounces ricotta

salt and pepper

PASTA

3 cups all-purpose flour

1 teaspoon salt

4 large eggs

2 tablespoons olive oil

pinch saffron

BROWN BUTTER SAUCE

4 ounces unsalted butter

4 sage leaves, thinly sliced

salt and pepper

2 ounces Parmesan cheese, shredded

1 tablespoon chives, chopped

To prepare the ravioli filling, add the butter to a large sauté pan and melt it over medium heat. Add the garlic and shallots and sauté them until they're golden. Add the lobster meat and chives, and sauté for 2-3 minutes. Deglaze the pan with the Chardonnay and reduce the liquid for 2 minutes. Remove the pan from the heat and allow the mixture to cool to room temperature, approximately 30 minutes. Chop the mixture into small chunks and combine with the ricotta. Season with salt and pepper and set aside.

To prepare the pasta, mix the flour and salt on a clean work surface. Make a well in the middle of the mixture and crack the eggs into the well. Add the olive oil and saffron and whisk with a fork until they are combined. Using the fork, incorporate the flour into the well a little at a time, until all the flour is mixed in. Knead the dough for 10 minutes, adding flour as needed to prevent sticking. Wrap the dough in a tea towel and let it sit for 30 minutes.

Cut the dough in ½ and roll out 1 piece using a pasta machine. Once the desired thickness is reached, brush the dough lightly with water or egg whites and place dollops of the lobster filling on the sheet, approximately 1 inch apart on all sides. Roll out the second piece of dough and place it gently on top of the first sheet. Using your fingers, press around each mound of filling to seal the dough. Cut the ravioli to size with a pastry cutter, and place them on a lightly floured sheet pan. Gently place the ravioli in boiling water and cook until they begin to float to the top.

Meanwhile, prepare the sauce by melting the butter in a large sauté pan over medium heat. Don't let it burn. When the butter turns brownish and gives off a nutty aroma, carefully drain the ravioli and add them to the pan. Add the sliced sage, season with salt and pepper, and toss to coat the ravioli. Transfer them to a serving dish and garnish with the shredded Parmesan and chives.

WHITE OAK VINEYARDS & WINERY

The family of our wine club manager, Alexandra Sartori, emigrated from Italy to Tomales Bay in the late 1860s. This hearty sauce is chef Dan Lucia's recreation of Alexandra's great grandmother's puttanesca recipe. Serve it over your favorite type of pasta.

7505 Highway 128 | Healdsburg, CA 95448
707-433-8429
whiteoakwinery.com

NONNA'S
PUTTANESCA SAUCE

Pair with White Oak Myers Reserve Red

SERVES 6-8

1 cup olive oil

6 cloves garlic

1 tablespoon red pepper flakes

½ cup kalamata olives, sliced

2 anchovies, minced

½ cup capers, drained

3 tablespoons tomato paste

3 cups tomatoes, finely chopped

1 cup fresh basil, chopped

In a pot, heat the olive oil over medium heat. Add the garlic, red pepper flakes, olives, anchovies and capers. Slowly cook them for 5 minutes.

Add the tomato paste, followed by the chopped tomatoes, and cook for 30 minutes.

Serve the sauce over cooked pasta and garnish with the basil.

ENTRÉES

Day of the Dead Oaxacan Turkey Mole

Savory Wild Mushroom Bread Pudding

Yummy AVV Chicken Stew

La Gare Duck a l'Orange

Fall Squash Pozole

Salmon Teriyaki Style

Zin-Marinated Steak Sandwich
with Onion Marmalade & Blue Cheese

Jacques Pépin's Sautéed Rabbit
with Morels & Pearl Onions

Mama's Sloppy Joe Sliders
with Shoestring Onion Rings

Alfonso's Italian Sausage with Grilled
Bread & Sautéed Vegetables

Spiced Duck with Herbed Couscous
& Sour Cherry Sauce

Grilled Portobello Mushrooms
with Warm Lentil Salad & Blue Cheese

Mama Fritz Truffled
White Bean Cassoulet

Pork Ragu over Fusilli Pasta

Red Wine-Braised Short Ribs

Roast Pork Tenderloin with Cabernet
Reduction & Caramelized Onions

Harvest Lamb Moussaka

Vote with Your Fork Polenta
with Walnuts & Rosemary Mushrooms

Baby Back Ribs with Spicy Sauce

Spaetzle with Lamb Meatballs &
Heirloom Tomato & Basil Brown Butter

Mushroom & Smoked Mozzarella Pizza

Duck Confit

Porchetta Italian Street Food

Slider Burger with Cabernet-Caramelized
Onions & Blue Cheese

Lizzy's Sweet & Savory Bacon &
Sausage Bean Chili

Meatballs with Late-Harvest
Heirloom Tomato Sauce

Pomegranate Pork Loin
with Heirloom Tomato
Chestnut Sauce & Quinoa Tabouleh

Brad's Dry-Rub Ribs

Zazu Short Rib Shepherd's Pie

Gourmet Mushroom Ragu
over Creamy Polenta

Really Goode Gumbo

Bison Meatballs with Warm
Cherry-Mushroom Rice Salad

Wild Boar Bolognese

Chicken Curry Stew

Perfect Sunday Pot Roast
with Rich Cabernet Gravy

Polpette e Polenta

Sweet T's Gumbo

Braised Pork with Herbed Polenta

Sweet Potato Cottage Pie

Le Boeuf de Bobcat

Pissaladière Skewis Style

Soda Rockin' Pork Chile Verde

Mediterranean Lamb Spear

Pearl Barley & Beef Stew

Denise's Famous
Pulled Pork Sandwiches

Winter Carnitas Tacos

Catelli's Meatballs

Bacon-Braised Beef Brisket

Aussie Paella with Herbie's Spices

Brandy-Infused Braised Pork
with Apples

Roasted Pork Shoulder with Saffron
Romesco & Crunchy Fried Chickpeas

ACORN WINERY/ALEGRIA VINEYARDS

I created this dish because my wife's birthday is November 2, one of the Days of the Dead. Days of the Dead honor those on the "other side," as many Mexicans believe that the door between earth and the dead is open on these two days; Oaxaca is home to some of the most colorful celebrations. The mole (MO-lay) recipe makes 2 quarts and freezes quite well. For Wine & Food Affair, we will serve the dish with mashed acorn squash and rayas.

12040 Old Redwood Hwy | Healdsburg, CA
707-433-6440
acornwinery.com

DAY OF THE DEAD

OAXACAN TURKEY MOLE

Pair with Acorn Heritage Vines Zinfandel

SERVES 6

4 ounces dried chiles negros
   (chiles mulato)

2 ounces dried ancho chiles

1 head garlic

1 Roma tomato

1 corn tortilla

¼ cup white sesame seeds

½ teaspoon cumin seeds

¾ cup corn oil

1 small yellow onion, sliced

¼ cup raw peanuts

¼ cup raw walnuts

¼ cup whole raw almonds

1 slice bread

1 ripe plantain

1-½ teaspoons dried oregano

1-½ teaspoons dried thyme

2 quarts chicken stock

¼ cup raisins

¾ teaspoon ground cinnamon

1 tablet Ibarra Mexican chocolate

salt and pepper, to taste

3 cups turkey meat, cooked

Destem the chiles, slit them open and remove the seeds. Toast the chiles in a dry skillet over medium-high heat. Set them aside.

Peel the papery skin from the garlic head. Roast it on a grill until it blackens, about 15 minutes, and remove the tough core and root. Char the whole tomato the same way. With tongs, char the tortilla over an open flame until it's well toasted. Let the tortilla cool, then grind it in a mortar. Remove the tortilla from the mortar. Toast the sesame and cumin seeds in a dry skillet over moderate heat, and grind them together in the mortar.

Heat a large skillet and add ½ cup of the oil and onion, cooking until the onion is caramelized. Remove the onions from the oil and set them aside. In the same skillet, add the nuts to the oil and fry them until they're golden brown. Remove the nuts and toast the bread on both sides in the skillet, then remove it. Add more oil, if necessary, and fry the plantain. Remove it from the pan.

Puree the chiles in a food processor with the garlic, sesame-cumin mix, oregano, thyme and 1 cup of chicken stock. Heat ¼ cup of oil in a clean skillet and add the puree. Cook for 20 minutes, stirring often to prevent sticking.

Puree in a blender the tortilla, onions, nuts, bread, plantain, raisins, cinnamon and 1 cup of stock. Combine this mixture with the chile mixture and remaining stock in a saucepan and cook over low heat for 15 minutes. Season to taste with salt and pepper, add the chocolate, and stir until it's melted.

To serve, place 2 cups of the mole in a saucepan and add the turkey. Heat them together, and serve over mashed acorn squash.

ALDERBROOK WINERY

Northern California is known as the best edible wild mushroom region in the world and this savory bread pudding features flavorful wild mushrooms in a way that works beautifully with wine. Served on its own with a bright green salad or as a lovely side dish to roasted pork or duck, this dish is sure to please everyone at the table.

2306 Magnolia Drive | Healdsburg, CA 95448
707-433-5987
alderbrook.com

VEGI

SAVORY WILD MUSHROOM
BREAD PUDDING

Pair with Alderbrook Russian River Valley Pinot Noir

SERVES 6

2 tablespoons unsalted butter, softened (plus extra to grease pan)

2 pounds assorted wild and cultivated mushrooms, sliced into evenly sized pieces

3 large eggs

1 cup whole milk

1 cup cream

2 teaspoons kosher salt

2 pinches freshly ground black pepper

1 pound brioche or challah loaf, cubed

4 ounces Gruyere cheese, grated

2 sprigs thyme, leaves only, finely chopped

½ tablespoon parsley, chopped

1 tablespoon Parmesan cheese, grated

Heat a sauté pan over medium-high heat and add 1 tablespoon of butter. Once it is bubbling, add the mushrooms in a single layer (cook in batches if necessary) and let them sear undisturbed, until they start to turn golden brown, about 3 minutes. Once the first side is browned, season the mushrooms with 1 teaspoon of kosher salt and a pinch of pepper, and sauté them they're golden brown all over, about 5 more minute. Transfer the mushrooms to a platter or bowl to cool.

Preheat oven to 400°.

Butter a 9-inch cast-iron pan or small casserole dish.

Whisk together the eggs, milk, cream, and remaining salt and pepper. Stir the mixture gently and add the cubed bread, sautéed mushrooms, Gruyere, thyme and parsley.

Transfer the mixture to the prepared pan or dish and press it down lightly to help the bread absorb the custard. Let stand for about 30 minutes.

Dot the top of the mixture with 1 tablespoon of softened butter and follow with a sprinkling of Parmesan. Bake the bread pudding until it's puffed and golden (not runny in the middle), about 30 minutes, and serve.

ALEXANDER VALLEY VINEYARDS

Chicken stew was always a Sunday treat at my grandmother's house. This is my take on her classic, and it's still my favorite comfort food — perfect for when I've been on the road and just want to come home and unwind. I'm continuing my grandmother's tradition and our grandsons love this dish as well. When I asked one what we should name it, he said, "Just call it yummy."

8644 Highway 128 | Healdsburg, CA 95448
707-433-7209
avvwine.com

YUMMY AVV
CHICKEN STEW

Pair with Alexander Valley Vineyards Estate Chardonnay

SERVES 6
STEW

7 cups chicken stock (if canned, use low salt/low fat)

1 bay leaf

2 tablespoons parsley, finely chopped

1 pound boneless skinless chicken thighs

2 tablespoons Wetzel Estate olive oil

¾ cup red onion, large dice

¾ cup celery, large dice

1 cup mushrooms, sliced

1-½ teaspoon AVV herbes de Provence

salt

pepper

2 cloves garlic, finely minced

½ cup AVV Chardonnay

8 tablespoons unsalted butter

⅔ cup flour

1 cup Yukon gold potatoes, large dice

1 cup carrots, large dice

½ teaspoon hot pepper sauce

10 ounces frozen peas

BISQUIT TOPPING

2 cups flour

2-½ teaspoons baking powder

1 teaspoon salt

2 teaspoons AVV herbes de Provence

½ cup Parmesan cheese, grated

¼ cup shortening

¾ cup milk

To prepare the stew, simmer the stock, bay leaf, 1 tablespoon of parsley and the chicken for 20 minutes. Remove the partially cooked chicken from the stock and cut it into bite-sized pieces. Reserve the stock.

In a sauté pan, heat the oil and cook the onion, celery, mushrooms, herbes de Provence and a pinch each of salt and pepper, until the vegetables are softened, about 5 minutes. Add the garlic and continue to sauté until the mixture is fragrant. Deglaze the pan with the wine and continue to cook until the liquid is reduced by ½. Set the pan aside.

In another sauté pan, melt the butter, stir in the flour and cook until the roux is pale yellow – not browned. Add the roux to the stock and whisk until all the ingredients are combined. Bring the pan to a boil, then reduce the heat to a simmer. Add the potatoes, carrots, sautéed vegetables, chicken, hot sauce, 1-½ teaspoons salt and ¼ teaspoon of pepper. Stir and simmer for 15-20 minutes.

Stir in the peas and remaining parsley. Pour the mixture into a buttered casserole dish.

To prepare the biscuit topping, preheat oven to 450°.

In a large bowl, blend the flour, baking powder, salt, herbes de Provence and ¼ cup of Parmesan. Add the shortening, and with a pastry cutter, work the mixture until it's in bits the size of peas. Add the milk and form the dough. Pat the dough into a ½-inch-thick circle (to match the casserole dish shape). Sprinkle the top of the dough with the remaining Parmesan and pat it again. Cut the dough into wedges and place each on top of the stew. Bake for 25-30 minutes, or until the stew is bubbly and the biscuits golden.

BALLETTO VINEYARDS

Roger Praplan, chef/owner of La Gare Restaurant in Santa Rosa, specializes in French country cooking. We called upon Roger to prepare this classic French dish, *canard à l'orange* – duck with orange sauce – to pair with our Pinot Noir. Bon appétit!

5700 Occidental Road | Santa Rosa, CA 95401
707-568-2455
ballettovineyards.com

LA GARE DUCK A L'ORANGE

Pair with Balletto Russian River Valley Pinot Noir

SERVES 2

¼ cup granulated sugar

2 tablespoons water

2 tablespoons sherry or
  red wine vinegar

1-½ cups chicken stock

¼ cup unsalted butter

1-½ cups orange juice

2 tablespoons shallots, minced

2 tablespoons orange zest

4 oranges, sections cut from
  membranes

2 duck breast halves, seasoned
  with salt and pepper

salt

pepper

¼ cup honey

In a saucepan, boil the sugar and water for several minutes, until the syrup caramelizes and turns golden brown. Deglaze the pan with the vinegar and continue to cook the syrup until it's reduced slightly. Add the orange juice and shallots and reduce by ½.

Add the chicken stock and simmer the mixture until the sauce is reduced to a little less than 1 cup. Add the butter and swirl it into the sauce. Stir in 1 tablespoon of the orange zest, then add the orange sections and immediately remove the pan from the heat. Set it aside.

Make small incisions on the fat side of the duck breast halves. Sprinkle them lightly with salt and pepper and lightly coat the fat side with honey. In a skillet, sear the duck breasts over high heat. Reduce the heat to medium and cook the duck for 9-11 minutes on each side (or bake at 350° for 6-8 minutes for medium rare).

To serve, slice the duck breasts on a bias. Spoon the orange sauce and orange segments on a serving platter and fan the duck breasts over the sauce. Garnish with the remaining orange zest scattered around the duck pieces.

BELLA VINEYARDS & WINE CAVES

This recipe is a Sonoma County take on a traditional Mexican comfort-food dish. The slight spiciness and varied texture of this hominy-driven stew makes it a perfect companion with Bella Zinfandel. The flavors of fall and a nod to California's past are incorporated in this seasonal pairing. It's best to marinate the pork in the spices 1 day in advance.

9711 West Dry Creek Road | Healdsburg, CA 95448
707-473-9171
bellawinery.com

FALL SQUASH POZOLE

Pair with Bella Belle Canyon Zinfandel

SERVES 6

2 tablespoons ground coriander

2 tablespoons ground fennel

1 tablespoon ground mustard

1 tablespoon powdered garlic

1 teaspoon cayenne pepper

1 teaspoon ground cinnamon

¼ cup paprika

1 tablespoon kosher salt

1 teaspoon black pepper

2 pounds pork shoulder, cut in
   1-inch cubes

canola oil

2 medium yellow onions, diced

3 carrots, rough cut about ½ inch

3 stalks celery, diced

4 cloves garlic, thinly sliced

2 bay leaves

1 8-ounce can diced green chilies

1 8-ounce can of Rotel diced
   tomatoes and chilies

2 cups dry white wine

1 28-ounce can Mexican-style white
   hominy (with liquid)

1 cup chicken stock

1 large butternut squash,
   diced ½ inch

1 bunch Italian parsley leaves,
   chopped

5 fresh sage leaves, chopped

One day ahead, mix all the dry spices (coriander through black pepper) in a bowl and toss with the pork cubes. Cover the bowl with foil and place it in the refrigerator overnight.

When you are ready to cook the pozole, heat a large, heavy-gauged stockpot over high heat. Coat the bottom with ⅛ inch of canola oil. Place enough of the pork in the pot to cover the bottom in 1 layer. Sear the meat on all sides, adjusting the heat and working quickly to make sure that the pan does not blacken. Remove the seared meat and add another batch, searing all the pork pieces and transferring them to a plate.

Immediately put the onions, carrots and celery into the pan and sauté them until they're translucent. Add the garlic, bay leaves, chilies and Rotel, and cook for 5 minutes more. Add the white wine and simmer until it evaporates halfway. Add the seared pork and the hominy with its liquid. Add the chicken stock, and bring the mixture to a boil. Turn the heat to medium low and cook the pork and vegetables together until the pork is tender, about 1 hour. Taste the stew occasionally and add salt or a little cayenne pepper, if desired.

Once the pork is cooked to perfection, add the butternut squash and cook for approximately ½ hour more, until the squash is tender. This stew, like most, is best served the day after it is made. When you're ready to serve it, bring the pozole to a simmer and add the chopped parsley and sage.

BLUENOSE WINES

My friends from Cape Breton Island, Nova Scotia, visit once a year and often bring fresh Atlantic salmon with them. Over time, we came up with this simple recipe for this delicious treat, often served with asparagus. Pacific salmon is a suitable substitute.

428 Hudson Street | Healdsburg, CA 95448
707-473-0768
bluenosewines.com

SALMON TERIYAKI STYLE

Pair with Bluenose Dry Creek Valley Zinfandel

SERVES 4

TERIYAKI SAUCE

½ cup soy sauce

¼ cup dry white wine

2 tablespoons brown sugar
  or honey

3-4 cloves garlic, to taste

1 teaspoon grated ginger

SALMON

1-½ teaspoons grated ginger

4 5-ounce wild salmon fillets

3-4 tablespoons butter

1 lemon, cut into wedges

Prepare the teriyaki sauce by mixing all the ingredients in a small bowl.

For the salmon, grate the ginger onto a large, shallow plate. Add ¼ cup teriyaki sauce and mix well. Remove the skin from the salmon fillets and place the fish on the plate. Marinate the fillets for 1 hour, turning them occasionally to coat both sides.

Melt the butter in a large sauté pan over medium heat. Cook the salmon 4-5 minutes per side, to desired doneness. Serve with lemon wedges on the side.

CAROL SHELTON WINES

During harvest, we often add to our crush team by inviting friends and wine club members to sort out leaves, punch down bins and clean up. Their reward is a tasty barbecue prepared by General Manager (and Carol's husband of 25 years) Mitch Mackenzie. One such meal included this marinated, grilled skirt steak and a zesty salad of arugula and blue cheese crumbles. Our friend and chef, Greg Hallihan, kicked the dish it up a notch by creating this sandwich. Start the recipe 1 day in advance.

3354-B Coffey Lane | Santa Rosa, CA 95403
707-575-3441
carolshelton.com

ZIN-MARINATED GRILLED
STEAK SANDWICH
WITH ONION MARMALADE & BLUE CHEESE

Pair with Carol Shelton Wild Thing Zinfandel

SERVES 8

STEAK

2 cups Carol Shelton Wild Thing Zin

½ red onion, sliced thin

4 cloves garlic, crushed and mashed

2 teaspoons olive oil

1 large skirt steak

CRÈME FRAÎCHE

1 cup sour cream

½ cup whipping cream

1-½ cups crumbled Point Reyes Blue Cheese

ONION MARMALADE

1 tablespoon olive oil

4 red onions, sliced

4 cups Wild Thing Zinfandel

1 cup sugar

SANDWICH

1 baguette

½ pound arugula, washed and dried

To prepare the steak marinade, mix the wine, red onion, garlic and olive oil in a large zip-sealing bag and add the skirt steak. Squeeze out the excess air, seal the bag and place it in the refrigerator overnight, turning the beef every 6 hours or so.

Also make the crème fraiche 1 day in advance. In a small bowl, mix the sour cream and whipping cream together and let the mixture sit for 24 hours in the refrigerator. The following day, fold in the blue cheese and mix well. (Leftovers can be refrigerated for up to 1 month.)

To prepare the sandwiches, first make the onion marmalade. Sauté the red onion slices in the olive oil for 5 minutes on medium heat. Add the Zinfandel and cook until the liquid is reduced by ½. Slowly add the sugar, stirring well, and simmer the marmalade for another 20 minutes on medium-low heat, until it thickens. Let it cool. (The recipe makes 2 cups, so you will likely have some to refrigerate for future use).

Grill the steak on a very hot grill for 4 minutes per side for rare, 1 minute or so longer for medium. Remove the meat from the grill and let it rest for 10 minutes, covered loosely with foil.

Slice the baguette lengthwise, then into quarters, for 8 open-face sandwiches. Thinly slice the steak. On each baguette slice, place a small handful of arugula leaves and slices of steak. Slather on the onion marmalade, and garnish with a dollop of blue cheese crème fraîche.

C. DONATIELLO WINERY

C. Donatiello was a sponsor of famed chef Jacques Pépin's "Essential Pépin" show on public television. In 2011, Pepin prepared this earthy, Pinot Noir-friendly rabbit dish for the program, and winery owner Chris Donatiello brings it to the 2013 Wine & Food Affair.

320 Center Street | Healdsburg, CA 95448
707-433-8285
cdonatiello.com

JACQUES PÉPIN'S

SAUTÉED RABBIT

WITH MORELS & PEARL ONIONS

Pair with C. Donatiello Russian River Valley Pinot Noir

SERVES 4

1 cup dried morel mushrooms

2 cups hot water

1 rabbit (about 3 pounds), cleaned and skinned

1 teaspoon herbes de Provence

¾ teaspoon salt

¼ teaspoon freshly ground black pepper

1 tablespoon unsalted butter

1 tablespoon plus 2 teaspoons olive oil

16 pearl onions

2 tablespoons shallots, chopped

1 tablespoon all-purpose flour

⅓ cup fruity, dry white wine

2 teaspoons garlic, chopped

1 tablespoon Dijon mustard

1 slice firm white bread

1 tablespoon bottled horseradish

Rinse the morels, put them in a bowl, and pour hot water over them. Submerge all the morels and let them soak for 30 minutes.

Cut the back legs from the rabbit and halve them at the joint. Remove the front legs. Remove the front part of the body that contains the rib cage, and cut this portion in ½. You now have 8 pieces plus the saddle, or back.

In a small bowl, mix the herbes de Provence, ½ teaspoon of the salt and the pepper. Sprinkle the saddle and rabbit pieces with the seasoning.

Heat the butter and 1 tablespoon of the oil in a Dutch oven. Add the rabbit saddle and pearl onions. Sauté them over medium-high heat, turning the saddle occasionally, until it and the onions are browned on all sides. Remove the saddle and set it aside. Transfer the onions to a bowl.

Add the rabbit pieces to the drippings in the pot, in 1 layer, and brown them on all sides, about 10 minutes.

Remove the morels from the soaking water and press them lightly to release their liquid back into the bowl. Cut them lengthwise. Pour the soaking liquid into a clean bowl, leaving behind any residue.

Add the shallots to the browning rabbit pieces, sprinkle the meat with flour, and mix gently. Cook for 1 minute. Add the wine, mushroom liquid, garlic and remaining salt, and mix well. Bring the pot to a boil, reduce the heat to low, and cover, cooking for 45 minutes.

Preheat oven to 425°.

Place the saddle on a foil-lined baking sheet and brush it with the mustard. Place the bread and horseradish in the bowl of a food processor and pulse until the mixture is finely ground. Add the remaining olive oil and mix to moisten the bread. Pat the mixture lightly over the top and sides of the saddle, so that it adheres to the mustard coating.

Roast the saddle for 20 minutes, and allow it to rest for 10 minutes. Add the morels and onions to the stew and cook them, covered, over low heat for 15 minutes.

To serve, divide the stew among 4 plates. Cut the saddle into 4 pieces and arrange them over the stew on each plate.

CHATEAU DIANA

You haven't had a Sloppy Joe until you've had one with buttermilk-fried shoestring onions topping the savory meat sauce. The crunchy, salty kick of the onions elevates the Sloppy Joe to new heights!

6195 Dry Creek Road | Healdsburg, CA 95448
707-433-6992
chateaud.com

MAMA'S SLOPPY JOE SLIDERS
WITH SHOESTRING ONION RINGS

Pair with Chateau Diana 707 Dry Creek Valley Old Vine Zinfandel

MAKES 8-10

SHOESTRING ONIONS

3 cups buttermilk
2 teaspoons hot sauce
1 egg, beaten
2 yellow onions, quartered and cut into ¼-inch strips
vegetable oil, for frying
2 cups self-rising flour
2 cups cornmeal
2 tablespoons garlic salt
½ teaspoon cayenne pepper

SLIDERS

2 tablespoons olive oil
1 small yellow onion, chopped
1 small red bell pepper, chopped
½ small jalapeno pepper, seeded and minced
1 7-ounce can chipotle peppers, drained and chopped
1-¼ pounds ground beef sirloin
1 tablespoon garlic, minced
2 cups tomato sauce
2 tablespoons tomato paste
2 tablespoons red wine vinegar
2 tablespoons red wine
1 tablespoon Worcestershire sauce
⅓ cup brown sugar
½ tablespoon paprika
½ tablespoon salt
½ tablespoon ground black pepper
½ teaspoon cayenne pepper
1 teaspoon cumin
½ teaspoon dry mustard
8 sliced slider buns, toasted

To prepare the shoestring onions, whisk together in a large bowl the buttermilk, hot sauce and egg. Add the onions and refrigerate the mixture for 30 minutes.

Meanwhile, prepare the slider filling by heating a large skillet over medium heat. Add the oil, onion, red pepper, jalapeno and chipotle peppers to the skillet. Sauté the vegetables until they're soft.

Add the ground beef and garlic, breaking up the beef with a wooden spoon, and cook until the meat is browned. Add the tomato sauce, tomato paste, vinegar, wine, Worcestershire, brown sugar, paprika, salt, black pepper, cayenne, cumin and mustard. Reduce the heat, cover and simmer the sauce on low heat for 30 minutes.

While the sauce cooks, remove the onions from the refrigerator. Fill a large pot or deep fryer ⅓ full with vegetable oil and heat it to 350°.

In a clean brown paper bag, combine the flour, cornmeal, 1 tablespoon of the garlic salt and ¼ teaspoon of the cayenne pepper. Drain the onion rings of their liquid and add them to the paper bag. Shake the bag until the onions are covered with the flour mixture, and let them sit for 5 minutes.

Gently add ½ of the onions to the hot oil and fry them, uncovered, for 4 minutes or until they're golden brown. Transfer the onions to paper towels to drain, and season them with ½ of the remaining garlic salt and cayenne. Fry, drain and season the second batch.

To serve, spoon the meat sauce onto the bottom ½ of each toasted bun, top with a haystack of onions, and add the top bun ½.

D'ARGENZIO WINERY

Our Wine & Food Affair recipes usually come from our Mama Rosa di Loiodice, yet this year, it's Alfonso A. D'Argenzio who weighs in with his grilled Italian sausages. Our family name, D'Argenzio, means "people of silver" in Italian, but this recipe is pure gold on our palates, and likely on yours, too. This dish is rustic and rewarding.

1301 Cleveland Avenue | Santa Rosa, CA 95401
707-546-2466
dargenziowine.com

ALFONSO'S ITALIAN SAUSAGE
WITH GRILLED BREAD & SAUTÉED VEGETABLES

Pair with D'Argenzio Dry Creek Valley Zinfandel

SERVES 4

1 pound Italian sausage links,
   mild or hot

1 bag sweet mini bell peppers,
   red, yellow and orange

1 head red cabbage

1 pound string beans

2 tablespoons olive oil

sea salt

black pepper

4 sourdough bread rolls

¼ cup Italian parsley, chopped

Preheat a grill to 300° and cook the sausages on it for 20 minutes, turning them occasionally. Set the browned sausages aside to cool, and cut them into ¼-inch-thick slices.

Slice the peppers into strips. Cut the cabbage into very thin wedges, keeping the layers intact. Place the pepper strips, cabbage wedges and the string beans on the grill. Brush them with 1 tablespoon of olive oil and season them with salt and pepper. Grill the vegetables 2-4 minutes per side.

Slice the bread rolls in ½ and brush them with the remaining olive oil. Season the bread with salt and pepper, and grill the slices for 2 minutes.

Place the sausage slices on the grilled bread, add the grilled vegetables, sprinkle the parsley on top, and serve.

DESMOND WINES

We are thrilled to showcase our Russian River Valley Estate Pinot Noir with this delicious recipe from a phenomenal chef. There aren't many better pairings than Pinot Noir and duck! Marinate the duck legs 1 day in advance.

3360 Coffey Lane | Santa Rosa, CA 95403
707-799-7449
desmondwines.com

SPICED DUCK
WITH HERBED COUSCOUS & SOUR CHERRY SAUCE

Pair with Desmond Estate Pinot Noir

SERVES 6-8

DUCK

2 teaspoons kosher salt

1 teaspoon ground allspice

1 teaspoon ground black pepper

½ teaspoon ground cloves

1 teaspoon ground cinnamon

8 Liberty Duck legs

3 cups Desmond Pinot Noir

1-½ cups dried sour cherries

1 yellow onion, diced

2 carrots, diced

3 celery ribs, diced

½ bunch fresh thyme

2 cloves garlic

1 quart canned tomatoes

6 quarts duck or chicken stock

COUSCOUS

⅓ cup fresh lemon juice

zest of 1 lemon

½ bunch cilantro

½ bunch parsley

1-½ cups olive oil

3 cups prepared plain couscous

⅓ cup pine nuts, toasted

1 cup sliced dinosaur kale

The night before you will prepare the dish, combine all of the spices and rub the mixture on both sides of the duck legs. Refrigerate overnight.

The next day, soak the cherries in 1 cup of the wine.

Preheat oven to 325°.

In a large pan, sauté the duck legs, onion, carrots, celery, garlic and thyme until the duck begins to brown and the vegetables start to soften. Add the tomatoes and remaining wine and sauté until the mixture is reduced by ½. Add the stock, cover the pan and cook the duck in the oven for 2 hours, or until the meat is tender.

Remove the legs to a platter and cover them loosely in foil to keep them warm. Strain the liquid in the pan and skim the fat from the surface. Return the liquid to the pan, add the cherries and their soaking liquid, and cook until the sauce is reduced by ½.

While the sauce reduces, prepare the couscous by adding the lemon juice, zest, cilantro and parsley to a blender. With the blender on, slowly add the olive oil to create a vinaigrette. Fluff the prepared couscous with a fork, add the vinaigrette, pine nuts and kale, and season with salt and pepper.

To serve, place a warm duck leg and a spoonful of couscous on each plate, and drizzle the sour cherry sauce over the duck.

FORCHINI VINEYARDS & WINERY

This dish was created after a good friend of ours became a vegetarian. Knowing she loves Cabernet Sauvignon, we wanted to serve a dish that had meaty flavor, yet without the meat. Portobello mushrooms provide that rich flavor that pairs so beautifully with Cabernet.

5141 Dry Creek Road | Healdsburg, CA 95448
707-431-8886
forchini.com

VEGI

GRILLED PORTOBELLO MUSHROOMS
WITH WARM LENTIL SALAD & POINT REYES BLUE CHEESE

Pair with Forchini Dry Creek Valley Cabernet Sauvignon

SERVES 6

MUSHROOMS
6 portobello mushrooms
2 tablespoons fresh thyme, minced
2 tablespoons shallots, minced
¼ cup red wine
1 tablespoon kosher salt
1 teaspoon black pepper
½ cup extra virgin olive oil
⅓ cup Point Reyes Blue Cheese, crumbled

LENTIL SALAD
¼ cup extra virgin olive oil
½ cup yellow onion, small dice
2 ribs celery, small dice
1 carrot, small dice
2 cloves garlic, minced
6 portobello mushroom stems, small dice
1-½ cups black beluga lentils, rinsed
kosher salt, to taste
1 bunch Italian flat leaf parsley, chopped

SHERRY VINAIGRETTE
¼ cup aged sherry vinegar
2 tablespoon Dijon mustard
1 small shallot, minced
1 tablespoon honey
½ cup canola oil
¼ cup extra virgin olive oil
kosher salt and fresh ground black pepper, to taste

Clean the mushrooms by removing their stems and scraping away the underside gills with a spoon. Set aside the stems for the lentil salad. With a sharp knife, score the tops of the mushrooms ¼-inch deep, in a crosshatch pattern. Transfer the mushrooms to a baking dish.

In a mixing bowl, combine the thyme, shallots, red wine, salt and pepper. Whisk in the olive oil. Pour the mixture over the mushrooms and rub it into the score marks. Marinate the mushrooms at room temperature while you prepare the lentils.

Heat a heavy saucepan over medium heat. Add the olive oil and sauté the onion, celery, carrot, garlic and mushroom stems until the onions are translucent. Add the lentils to the pan and cover them with water.

Bring the lentils to a boil, then reduce the heat to a simmer and cook the lentils 40-45 minutes, or until they're just tender. Season them to taste with kosher salt, drain the remaining water, and keep the lentils warm.

While the lentils cook, prepare the vinaigrette by whisking all the ingredients together in a small bowl. Season to taste with salt and pepper.

When you are ready to serve the dish, grill the mushrooms until they're cooked through. Set them aside and keep them warm.

Toss the lentils with the vinaigrette and chopped parsley. Slice the mushrooms and place them over the lentils. Sprinkle the mushrooms with the crumbled blue cheese.

FRITZ UNDERGROUND WINERY

On cold winter nights, there is nothing better than a warm white-bean cassoulet with duck confit. A hint of truffle elevates the casserole to a higher level.

24691 Dutcher Creek Road | Cloverdale, CA 95425
707-894-3389
fritzwinery.com

MAMA FRITZ

TRUFFLED WHITE BEAN CASSOULET

Pair with Fritz Russian River Valley Pinot Noir

SERVES 6

2 cups dried navy beans, soaked in water overnight

6 cups chicken stock plus 1 cup reserved

3 sprigs thyme

1 bay leaf

½ cup garlic cloves, peeled

1 yellow onion, diced

black pepper

2 blood sausage links

2 duck confit legs, shredded

½ cup panko bread crumbs

2 tablespoons white truffle oil

3 tablespoons fresh parsley

Drain the soaked beans and place them in a pot large enough to hold them and the chicken stock. Bring the stock and beans to a simmer, stirring occasionally, then add the thyme, bay leaf, garlic, onion and a few grinds of black pepper. Continue to simmer the mixture until most of the stock has been absorbed and the beans are tender, approximately 50 minutes. Add water or stock if the liquid evaporates before the beans are cooked through.

Meanwhile, bring the extra cup of chicken stock to a simmer in a saucepan and poach the sausage links in it for 8-10 minutes. Remove the links and add the remaining stock to the beans, if needed.

Preheat oven to 400°.

When the beans are tender, place them a casserole dish or individual ramekins. Slice the sausage links 1-inch thick, scatter them throughout the beans, and do the same with the shredded duck.

Sprinkle the casserole or ramekins with the bread crumbs and truffle oil, and bake them the oven, until their tops are golden brown and bubbling. Garnish with the parsley and serve.

GEYSER PEAK WINERY

After all the hard work of harvest
is over, and the evenings begin to cool
as we head into winter, this is the
perfect hearty dish for the season.

22281 Chianti Road | Geyserville, CA 95441
707-857-2500
geyserpeakwinery.com

PORK RAGU OVER FUSILLI PASTA

Pair with Geyser Peak Walking Tree Cabernet Sauvignon

SERVES 8

¼ cup olive oil

4 tablespoons butter

8 cloves garlic, minced

½ cup carrots, diced

1 cup onion, diced

½ cup celery, diced

3-½ pound ground pork shoulder

1-½ cups Walking Tree Cabernet Sauvignon

salt and pepper, to taste

2 teaspoons nutmeg

1 cup milk

2 cups chicken stock

4 cups tomato puree

1 cup heavy cream

1 package dried fusilli pasta

6 ounces ricotta salata, grated

½ cup parsley, chopped

In a large pot, heat the olive oil and butter. Add the garlic, carrots, onion and celery, and sauté until the vegetables are soft, 8-10 minutes. Add the ground pork and brown the meat.

Add the wine to the pot and cook to reduce the liquid by ½. Season the pork with salt, pepper and nutmeg, and add the milk, stock and tomato puree. Slowly cook the sauce for approximately 1 hour, or until it becomes thick. Add the heavy cream and bring the mixture to a gentle simmer.

Cook the fusilli according to package directions and drain the pasta well. Spoon the the sauce over the fusilli and garnished with the ricotta salata and chopped parsley.

GRATON RIDGE CELLARS

We love short ribs here at Graton Ridge Cellars!
Braised in red wine, these tasty bites will melt
in your mouth and are perfectly paired with
our earthy Russian River Valley Pinot Noir.
You're gonna need a napkin – or five!

3561 Gravenstein Highway North | Sebastopol, CA 95472
707-823-3040
gratonridge.com

RED WINE-BRAISED SHORT RIBS

Pair with Graton Ridge Russian River Valley Pinot Noir

SERVES 6

5 pounds bone-in beef short ribs, cut crosswise into 2-inch pieces

kosher salt and freshly ground black pepper

3 tablespoons vegetable oil

3 medium onions, chopped

3 medium carrots, peeled and chopped

2 celery stalks, chopped

3 tablespoons all-purpose flour

1 tablespoon tomato paste

1 750 ml bottle Graton Ridge Pinot Noir

10 sprigs flat leaf parsley

8 sprigs thyme

4 sprigs oregano

2 sprigs rosemary

2 dried bay leaves

1 head garlic, halved crosswise

4 cups low-salt beef stock

Season the short ribs with salt and pepper. Heat the oil in a large Dutch oven over medium-high heat. Working in 2 batches, brown the ribs on all sides, about 8 minutes per batch. Transfer the ribs to a plate. Pour off all but 3 tablespoons of the drippings in the pot.

Add the onions, carrots and celery to the pot and cook them over medium-high heat, stirring often, until the onions are browned, about 5 minutes. Add the flour and tomato paste; cook, stirring constantly, until the ingredients are combined and a deep red, 2-3 minutes.

Stir in the wine, and add the short ribs and their accumulated juices. Bring the mixture to a boil, lower the heat to medium, and simmer until the wine is reduced by ½, about 25 minutes.

Preheat oven to 350°.

Add all the herbs to the pot, along with the garlic. Stir in the beef stock. Bring the pot to a boil, cover it, and place it in the oven. Cook until the ribs are tender, about 2-2-½ hours.

Transfer the ribs to a platter. Strain the sauce from the pot into a measuring cup. Spoon the fat from the surface of the sauce and discard it. Season the sauce to taste with salt and pepper. Serve ribs in shallow bowls over mashed potatoes, and spoon the sauce over the ribs.

GUSTAFSON FAMILY VINEYARDS

This is a relatively quick and easy meal, and if you double the recipe, you can have one hearty dinner and a week's supply of the best sandwich meat on the planet. We cook one up every week or so during harvest, and even if we don't have time to get fancy with the onions and baguette, it's still downright delicious. We simply haven't found a better match for our Cabernet. Be sure to marinate the pork the night before you plan to serve it.

9100 Stewarts Point-Skaggs Springs Road
Geyserville, CA 95441
707-433-2371
gfvineyard.com

ROAST PORK TENDERLOIN
WITH CABERNET REDUCTION & CARAMELIZED ONIONS

Pair with Gustafson Estate Cabernet Sauvignon

SERVES 6

PORK

1 3-pound center-cut pork
tenderloin, fat and silver
skin removed

¼ cup balsamic vinegar

2 tablespoons salt

1 small onion, diced

2 cloves garlic, minced

½ cup olive oil plus more
for searing

1 tablespoon fresh ground
pepper

1 rustic baguette

REDUCTION/ONIONS

4 large onions, cut into
matchsticks

1 cup olive oil

½ tablespoon sugar

2 tablespoons balsamic vinegar

1 bottle Gustafson Cabernet
Sauvignon

4 tablespoons butter

The night before, place the tenderloin in a shallow baking dish and let it stand at room temperature for 15 minutes. Add the vinegar, salt, onion and garlic to the pan and coat the pork in the mixture. After 15 minutes, add the olive oil and pepper. Place the tenderloin and marinade in a zip-closure plastic bag and refrigerate it overnight.

The next day, prepare the reduction sauce by sautéing the onions in the olive oil over low heat for 20-30 minutes. When the onions begin to brown, add the sugar and vinegar and continue to sauté until the onions are caramelized.

Preheat oven to 425°.

Remove the pork from the refrigerator and discard the marinade. Heat a small amount of oil in a large sauté pan and sear the tenderloin on all sides, until it is lightly browned. Place the loin in a roasting pan and cook it in the oven to internal temperature of 120-125°, about 15 minutes. Remove the loin from the oven and allow it to rest for 15 minutes. Reserve the pan drippings.

Heat the wine in an uncovered saucepan over medium heat, and reduce it to ⅓. Add 1 cup of the drippings from the pork roasting pan. Blend in the butter, and season with salt and pepper to taste.

To serve, slice the tenderloin into thin strips and place them on slices of baguette. Top with the caramelized onions and Cabernet reduction.

HANNA WINERY & VINEYARDS

I adore this dish in the winter, with our hearty Cabernet Sauvignon. It's a make-ahead dish that tastes great the next day, and is perfect for a party.

9280 Highway 128
Healdsburg, CA 95448
707-431-4310

5353 Occidental Road
Santa Rosa, CA 95401
707-575-3371

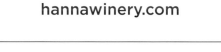

hannawinery.com

HARVEST LAMB MOUSSAKA

Pair with Hanna Alexander Valley Cabernet Sauvignon

SERVES 12

EGGPLANT

2 globe eggplants, cut crosswise into ½-inch slices

3 tablespoons olive oil

LAMB

1 tablespoon olive oil

1 large onion, chopped fine

2 pounds ground lamb

2 garlic cloves, minced

1 tablespoon salt

1 teaspoon fresh ground pepper

1 teaspoon oregano

2 cups fresh tomatoes, chopped (or canned if not in season)

TOPPING

4 large eggs

1 cup plain yogurt

2 cups lukewarm low-fat milk

1 teaspoon hot paprika

½ cup Parmiggiano Reggiano, grated

Preheat oven to 375°.

Place the eggplant slices in a single layer on an oiled baking sheet. Brush the tops with the olive oil and roast them until they're tender. Keep the oven temperature at 375°.

To prepare the lamb, sauté the onions in olive oil until they're translucent. Add the lamb and garlic, and continue to sauté until the lamb is browned. Add the salt, pepper and oregano.

In a separate bowl, beat all of the topping ingredients except for the Parmiggiano Reggiano.

Layer the roasted eggplant slices, meat mixture and tomatoes in a gratin or glass baking dish. Pour the topping over the layers and sprinkle the top with the grated cheese.

Bake the moussaka for 30-45 minutes, until the top is set and slightly browned. Let it cool for 10 minutes, cut into squares and serve.

HART'S DESIRE WINE

In a family winery, it's always go, go, go! Desire Hart is in charge of making sure we slow down and stay healthy. She came up with this recipe after she made a fall trip to our local farmers market. We aren't in the "no" business and offer a vegan, gluten-free dish every year at Wine & Food Affair, so that all of our friends can enjoy it with us.

53 Front Street | Healdsburg, CA 95448
707-433-3097
hartsdesirewines.com

VEGI

VOTE WITH YOUR FORK POLENTA
WITH WALNUTS & ROSEMARY MUSHROOMS

Pair with Hart's Desire Alexander Valley Viognier

SERVES 6

1-2 tablespoons coconut oil

8 ounces walnut pieces

salt and pepper, to taste

8 ounces mushrooms, sliced

1 teaspoon rosemary

3 cups vegetable broth

1 cup coconut milk
  (not coconut water)

1 cup dry polenta

Preheat oven to 400°.

Heat 1 tablespoon of coconut oil in a saucepan and add the walnuts, salt and pepper. Cook the walnuts, stirring continuously, until they begin to bronze. Transfer them to a sheet pan and toast them in the oven until they are evenly browned. Set the walnuts aside.

Prepare the rosemary mushrooms by heating 1 tablespoon of coconut oil in a sauté pan over medium heat. Add the mushrooms in 1 layer and cook them without stirring, until they're caramelized. Flip the mushrooms over, add the rosemary, and cook the other side until the mushrooms are fully caramelized. Season with salt and pepper and stir to mix well.

To prepare the polenta, place the broth and coconut milk in a saucepan and bring them to a hard simmer. Pour in the dry polenta, whisking continuously to prevent clumping. Reduce the heat and cover the saucepan, removing it only to stir the mixture often. The polenta is done when it begins to pull away from the sides of the pan.

Mix the walnuts and rosemary mushrooms into the polenta and serve.

J. KEVERSON WINERY

A few years ago our daughter made some barbecue sauce for John for Father's Day. He loved it and has recreated it many times. His is a much spicier version, of course! John likes this sauce on barbecued ribs, but it also goes great with chicken and steak.

53 Front Street | Healdsburg, CA 95448
707-433-3097
jkeverson.com

BABY BACK RIBS
WITH SPICY SAUCE

Pair with J. Keverson Starkey's Court Zinfandel

SERVES 6-8

RIBS

2 slabs baby back ribs

2 tablespoons olive oil

salt and freshly ground black pepper

SAUCE

3 teaspoons extra virgin olive oil

⅓ cup garlic, minced

2 cups Zinfandel

⅔ cup white balsamic vinegar

24 ounces ketchup

1 tablespoon Grey Poupon Dijon mustard

2 teaspoons Asian chili sauce

1 cup brown sugar

2 tablespoons honey

2 teaspoons cumin powder

2 teaspoons chili powder

1 teaspoon freshly ground black pepper

Preheat oven to 225°.

Brush the olive oil on both sides of the ribs. Sprinkle them with salt and pepper on both sides. Place the ribs on foil-lined, rimmed baking sheets and cook them for 2-½ hours.

While the ribs cook, prepare the sauce. In a large stockpot or Dutch oven, heat the olive oil over medium-high heat and add the garlic. Sauté the garlic for about 5 minutes, until it's fragrant and slightly soft.

Add the remaining ingredients and bring the mixture to a boil. Reduce the heat to a simmer and cook, uncovered, until the sauce thickens, about 1-1-½ hours. Stir the sauce occasionally to prevent it from scorching.

Remove the pan from the heat and let the sauce cool. Store it in the refrigerator until the ribs are done.

Prepare a grill for indirect heat. Place the baked ribs on the grill. Reserve some of the barbecue sauce for serving. Baste the remaining sauce on both sides of the ribs and grill them for 30-45 minutes. Serve the reserved sauce with the ribs.

KACHINA VINEYARDS

We couldn't pronounce spaetzle, let alone spell it, but when we paired it with lamb meatballs and our Cabernet Sauvignon, we knew we had to 'noodle' this. Spaetzle is a cross between a noodle and a dumpling. It's a culinary delight common in Germany, yet we also enjoy it in Sonoma wine country.

4551 Dry Creek Road | Healdsburg, CA 95448
707-332-7917
kachinavineyards.com

SPAETZLE WITH LAMB MEATBALLS
AND HEIRLOOM TOMATO & BASIL BROWN BUTTER

Pair with Kachina Dry Creek Valley Cabernet Sauvignon

SERVES 8

MEATBALLS

2 pounds ground lamb

1 pound ground pork

¼ cup toasted bread crumbs

3 eggs

1 tablespoon parsley, chopped

1 tablespoon smoked sea salt

1 tablespoon ground black
   pepper

SPAETZLE

2 cups all-purpose flour

1 teaspoon ground nutmeg

1-½ teaspoons ground black
   pepper

1 teaspoon kosher salt

4 eggs

½ cup whole milk

4 tablespoons butter

1 tablespoon garlic, chopped

4 tablespoons basil, chopped

1 cup heirloom tomatoes,
   chopped

To prepare the meatballs, first preheat the oven to 375°.

Mix all the ingredients in a large bowl. Form 2-ounce meatballs with your hands and place them on a baking sheet. Bake the meatballs in the oven to medium doneness, approximately 8 minutes. Set them aside to cool.

Prepare the spaetzle by bringing 2 gallons of water to a boil on the stovetop. Mix together the flour, nutmeg, pepper and salt in a large bowl. Beat the eggs in a small bowl and add them to the dry ingredients, alternating with the milk. Mix until the dough is smooth. Press the dough through a large-holed sieve or metal grater to form the spaetzle.

Drop the spaetzle, a few at a time, into the boiling water. Cook them for 6 minutes and drain them well.

Brown the butter in a sauté pan. Add the cooked spaetzle, garlic, basil and tomatoes. Stir to combine, season with salt and pepper, and serve with a meatball.

KENDALL-JACKSON WINE CENTER

The combination of mushrooms and smoked mozzarella is wonderful paired with our rich and earthy Cabernet Sauvignon. We like to use Cabernet in our house-made pizza sauce, to further bridge the flavors of the dish to the wine, but you can use your own favorite sauce for this dish.

5007 Fulton Road | Fulton, CA 95439
707-571-8100
kj.com

VEGI

MUSHROOM & SMOKED MOZZARELLA
PIZZA

Pair with Kendall-Jackson Grand Reserve Cabernet Sauvignon

SERVES 4

2 cups plus 2 tablespoons lukewarm water (not hot)

1 pack Fleishmann's dry active yeast

⅛ teaspoon sugar

1 tablespoon olive oil plus 1 tablespoon for oiling pan

¼ cup plus 1 tablespoon semolina flour

¼ cup wheat flour

4 cups unbleached bread flour

1-½ teaspoons kosher salt

2 cups pizza sauce

2 pounds smoked mozzarella, cut into ¼-inch thick circles

1 pound mushrooms, sliced

To prepare the dough, use an electric mixer fitted with a dough hook attachment. To the bowl of the mixer, add 1 cup plus 1 tablespoon of lukewarm water, the yeast, sugar and olive oil. Mix for a few seconds and let the dough stand for 5 minutes.

Place the semolina, wheat and unbleached flours in the bowl, on top of the water, and mix them, adding in the remaining water and the salt. Knead the dough on the first speed for approximately 3 minutes, or until a rough dough begins to form.

Transfer the dough to a floured work surface and knead it for 1-2 minutes with your hands, being careful not to add too much flour; the dough will be sticky and wet, and this is good. Lightly oil the inside of a large bowl and place the dough inside. Loosely cover the bowl with plastic wrap and let the dough proof in a draft-free spot at room temperature for approximately 1 hour, or until it doubles in size.

Transfer the dough again to a lightly floured work surface and divide it into 4 equal pieces. Form each piece into a ball, being careful not to deflate the dough. Let the balls rest on the work surface for 20 minutes, loosely covered with plastic wrap.

Preheat oven to 500⁰.

Generously drizzle the center of a baking sheet with olive oil. Place a dough ball on the oil and begin to work the dough into a flat circle from the inside out. When the pizza dough is about ½ the final size, flip it over and work the dough until it extends to 10-12 inches.

Top the dough with a thin layer pizza sauce, leaving a ½-inch border. Top the sauce with the mozzarella and mushrooms. Repeat this process with the remaining dough. Bake each pizza for 12 minutes or until the dough is browned and the cheese is melted. Rotate the pan halfway through.

LA CREMA TASTING ROOM

Use this flavorful duck confit in your favorite dishes, such as duck rillettes, stew, pasta or seared with a frisée salad. We pair it with Pinot Noir, as the earthiness of the wine is wonderful with the richness of the duck. Start this dish one day in advance.

235 Healdsburg Avenue | Healdsburg, CA 95448
707-431-9400
lacrema.com

DUCK CONFIT

Pair with La Crema Pinot Noir

SERVES 6-8

6 duck legs, thighs attached

½ pound kosher salt

5 sprigs fresh thyme

1 tablespoon whole black peppercorns

¼ pound sugar

1 tablespoon fennel seeds

1 bay leaf

1 tablespoon juniper berries

1 quart duck fat

Place the duck legs in a non-reactive perforated container. Evenly distribute the legs and coat them with all of the ingredients except for the duck fat. Cover the legs with plastic wrap and place a weight on top of the wrap. Refrigerate the legs overnight.

The next day, preheat oven to 275°.

Rinse the duck in cold water and pat the legs dry with paper towels. Place them in an ovenproof pan and cover them with duck fat. Cover the pan with aluminum foil and place it in the oven. Cook the duck until the meat is tender and falling off of the bone, about 2½ hours.

Remove the duck from the oven and let it cool. Pick the meat off the bones and shred it with 2 forks. Discard any bones, fat, skin or gristle. Serve the confit right away, with your favorite dishes, or store it, covered, with melted duck fat in the refrigerator.

LOCALS TASTING ROOM

When I lived in Tuscany, one of my favorite stops on my Vespa 125 was a small porchetta truck on my way home to Bocca Di Magra. The truck came once a week, on Thursdays, and I would always make a stop. This recipe is my take on this Italian street food. Start this recipe one day in advance.

21023-A Geyserville Avenue | Geyserville, CA 95441
707-857-4900
tastelocalwines.com

PORCHETTA ITALIAN STREET FOOD

Pair with Locals Zinfandel

SERVES 12-15

1 6-pound fresh pork belly, skin on

1 3-pound boneless, center-cut pork loin, trimmed

4 tablespoons fennel seeds or pollen

2 tablespoons red pepper flakes

2 tablespoons fresh sage, minced

1 tablespoon fresh rosemary, minced

3 garlic cloves, minced

kosher salt

black pepper

Place the pork belly on a work surface, skin side down, and place the loin in the center. Roll the belly around the loin so that the short ends of the belly meet. If any of the belly or loin overhangs, trim the excess. Unroll the belly and loin.

Refrigerate the pork, uncovered, for 1 day to allow the skin to air-dry; pat it occasionally with paper towels.

The next day, remove the porchetta from the refrigerator and let it sit at room temperature for 2 hours. While the porchetta rests, toast the fennel seeds and red pepper flakes in a small skillet until they're fragrant, about 1 minute. Tip them into a spice grinder and let them cool. Finely grind the fennel and pepper flakes, and transfer them to a small bowl along with the sage, rosemary and garlic.

Preheat oven to 500°.

Place the belly skin side down on a clean work surface. Using a knife, score the flesh in a checkerboard pattern, ⅓-inch deep, so that the roast will cook evenly. Turn the belly skin side up. Using a paring knife, poke dozens of ⅛-inch-deep holes through the skin. Using a meat mallet, pound the skin for 3 minutes to tenderize the meat.

Turn the belly and generously salt both it and loin. Rub both pieces with the fennel-spice mixture. Arrange the loin down the middle of the belly. Roll the belly around the loin and tie it crosswise with kitchen twine, at ½-inch intervals. Trim the twine, and transfer the pork to a wire rack set inside a rimmed baking sheet.

Roast the pork for 40 minutes, then turn the meat over. Reduce the heat to 300° and continue roasting, rotating the pan and turning the porchetta occasionally, until an instant-read thermometer inserted into the center of the meat registers 145°, about 1-½ to 2 hours more. If the skin is not yet deep brown and crisp, increase the heat to 500° and roast for 10 minutes more.

Let the porchetta rest for 30 minutes. Using a serrated knife, slice it into ½-inch rounds and serve.

MARTIN RAY WINERY

This entrée is simple, easy and fun to eat. The caramelized onions and blue cheese pair beautifully with Cabernet Sauvignon. Use a high-quality, sharp blue such as local Point Reyes Farmstead Blue, and excellent-quality grass-fed beef. The recipe for the caramelized onions yields more that you need for the burgers, and the onions will keep, refrigerated, for a few weeks, for use on sandwiches, grilled chicken and steak.

2191 Laguna Road | Santa Rosa, CA 95401
707-823-2404
martinraywinery.com

SLIDER BURGER
WITH CABERNET-CARAMELIZED ONIONS & BLUE CHEESE

Pair with Martin Ray Sonoma County Cabernet Sauvignon

SERVES 8

CARAMELIZED ONIONS

4 medium red onions, peeled and thinly sliced

2 cups Martin Ray Cabernet Sauvignon

½ cup sugar

2 tablespoons balsamic vinegar

2 bay leaves

pinch salt

pinch cayenne pepper

SLIDERS

1-½ pounds ground beef (18-20%)

kosher salt, to taste

8 grinds black pepper

1 teaspoon rosemary, chopped

8 small potato rolls

¼ pound Point Reyes Blue Cheese

To prepare the onions, place all the ingredients in a heavy-bottomed sauce pot. Turn the heat to high, cover the pot tightly, and simmer the mixture for 15 minutes. Lower the heat to medium-high, remove the cover and continue cooking the onions for about 45 minutes, stirring occasionally. As the liquid starts to thicken, lower the heat and stir the onions with a wooden spoon until it is almost all evaporated. Allow the mixture to cool. Taste and add salt if needed. Keep the onions warm while you prepare the sliders; leftovers can be stored in a glass jar in the refrigerator.

Prepare the sliders by forming the ground beef into small patties that are approximately 3 ounces each. Press them gently so that they remain tender. Sprinkle both sides with salt, pepper and rosemary. Preheat a grill to medium-hot. Rub a little oil on the grill and then cook the burgers to medium-rare.

While the burgers are cooking, split the rolls in ½ and toast them on the corner of the grill. Place 1 cooked slider burger on each bun bottom. Top each with blue cheese first, then the warm onions and the bun top.

MARTINELLI WINERY

It all started with an innocent present brought home to a husband. "Look, honey, I got you an Easter pig!" He named her Elizabeth, after his little sister, but we called her Lizzy. She frolicked in her pen, and if you scratched her back, she would squeal, wiggle and jump in the air. It was really fun ... until she grew to 500 pounds. It was time, though it wasn't easy. My husband, the tough guy, had a butcher do the deed. And we had to come up with recipes that used pork – and lots of it! This is one of the most delicious.

3360 River Road | Windsor, CA 95492
707-525-0570
martinelliwinery.com

LIZZY'S SWEET & SAVORY
BEAN CHILI WITH BACON & SAUSAGE

Pair with Martinelli Vigneto di Evo Zinfandel

MAKES 1 GALLON

1-½ pounds bacon, sliced

1-½ pounds Portuguese or spicy Italian sausage, without casing

1 onion, chopped

1 tablespoon garlic, crushed

1 6-ounce can tomato paste

1 15-ounce can stewed tomatoes

1 15-ounce can tomato sauce

¼ cup molasses

½ cup brown sugar

2 teaspoons Worcestershire sauce

1 15-ounce can pinto beans, drained

1 15-ounce can kidney beans, drained

1 15-ounce can butter beans, drained

1 15-ounce can white kidney beans, drained

1 12-ounce bottle/can beer

Cut the bacon into 1-inch strips and cook it in a Dutch oven until the bacon is crispy. Let the strips drain on a paper towel.

Remove the bacon fat from the Dutch oven and add the sausage meat, onion and garlic. Cook until the meat is nicely browned throughout. Drain off any excess fat.

Put the bacon strips back into the pot, along with all the rest of the ingredients, and bring the mixture to a slow simmer. Cook the chili for 2-3 hours, stirring occasionally. If it seems too thick, add more beer. If it seems too thin, add more tomato paste.

Serve with a side of cornbread.

MARTORANA FAMILY WINERY

These saucy meatballs are wonderful when served over your favorite pasta or polenta. California heirloom tomatoes are usually available through November; if you can't find them, buy the freshest, vine-ripened tomatoes possible.

5956 West Dry Creek Road | Healdsburg, CA 95448
707-433-1909
martoranafamilywinery.com

MEATBALLS
WITH LATE-HARVEST HEIRLOOM TOMATO SAUCE

Pair with Martorana Dry Creek Valley Zinfandel

SERVES 6-8

SAUCE

4 tablespoons olive oil

⅓ cup onion, diced

⅓ cup celery, diced

5 garlic cloves, minced

1 cup Martorana Zinfandel

8 cups heirloom tomatoes, diced

4 tablespoons butter

½ cup basil, chopped

MEATBALLS

3 pounds ground beef

3 pounds ground pork

1 cup onion, diced

⅓ cup garlic, chopped

1 tablespoon red pepper flakes

1 cup sourdough bread, soaked in milk

½ cup Parmesan cheese, grated

2 eggs

⅓ cup fresh oregano, chopped

⅓ cup parsley, chopped

Preheat oven to 350°.

First prepare the sauce by placing the olive oil in a saucepan and warming it over medium heat. Add the onion, celery and garlic, and sauté the vegetables for 5 minutes. Add the Zinfandel and continue to cook until the liquid is reduced by ¼. Add the tomatoes and cook the sauce for approximately 1 hour.

While the sauce cooks, prepare the meatballs. Combine all the ingredients in a large missing bowl. Form the mixture into 16 meatballs. Place them on a sheet pan and bake them in the oven for 30 minutes.

Remove the sauce from the stove and allow it to cool slightly. With an immersion blender, process the sauce until it's smooth, then add the butter. Stir the sauce to combine the butter, and season with salt and pepper.

Serve the sauce over the meatballs, garnished with the chopped basil.

MATRIX WINERY

Radio Africa & Kitchen chef Eskender Aseged has developed the perfect recipe for a crisp fall evening and a marriage with winemaker Diane Wilson's Pinot Noirs. Drawing on local ingredients, this is a recipe that epitomizes Sonoma County at its finest.

3291 Westside Road | Healdsburg, CA 95448
707-433-1911
matrixwinery.com

POMEGRANATE PORK LOIN
WITH HEIRLOOM TOMATO CHESTNUT SAUCE & QUINOA TABOULEH

Pair with Matrix Bacigalupi Vineyard Pinot Noir

SERVES 6

PORK
4 tablespoons pomegranate juice
1 tablespoon lemon juice
2 teaspoons salt
2 teaspoons ground pepper
2 tablespoons extra virgin olive oil
2 pounds pork loin

TOMATO SAUCE
2 pounds Sonoma heirloom tomatoes,
   seeded and diced
2 tablespoons garlic, crushed
2 tablespoons shallots, crushed
2 teaspoons cinnamon
2 teaspoons cardamom
2 teaspoons cumin
2 tablespoons red pepper flakes
4 tablespoons orange blossom honey
4 tablespoons extra virgin olive oil
pinch of saffron
salt and pepper, to taste
1 cup roasted chestnuts, finely chopped

TABOULEH
3 cups water
2 cups uncooked quinoa
drizzle olive oil
4 teaspoons cumin
1 cup cooked garbanzo beans
1 cup flat leaf parsley
2 teaspoons garlic
2 tablespoons shallots, chopped
¼ cup lemon juice

Combine the pork ingredients in a glass baking dish and marinate the meat for a minimum of 20 minutes or up to 2 hours.

In a heavy-bottom saucepan, mix all of the tomato sauce ingredients together except for the chestnuts. Bring the mixture to a simmer over medium heat and cook for 2 hours. Let the sauce cool, then add the chopped chestnuts.

Preheat grill.

Preheat oven to 350°.

Prepare the tabouleh by placing the water and quinoa in a saucepan. Add a drizzle of olive oil and let the quinoa simmer on low heat for 8 minutes. Let it cool. Add the remaining tabouleh ingredients to the quinoa and gently stir. Set the pan aside so that the flavors meld.

Remove the pork from the marinade and grill it on all sides. Transfer the meat to the oven and cook it through, approximately 12 minutes, or until the meat is medium or 145° in the center. Allow the meat to rest for a few minutes before slicing it.

Plate the pork slices, add a dollop of tomato sauce over the meat, and serve with the tabouleh.

MERCURY WINE GEYSERVILLE

I got this recipe 25 years ago from a stubborn Southern gentleman who wouldn't share it until he considered me worthy. My Navy buddy, Dr. Charlie Jones, invited me to his family's annual Memorial Day barbecue. His Uncle Steve was in charge of the ribs, and I fell in love with them. I asked Steve for the recipe, and I was denied, not just in the first year, but also the second and third. In the fourth year, Uncle Steve finally told me the secret to his ribs, and I'm sharing it with you. The key is in the grilling method, and giving yourself plenty of time to cook the ribs. When you have a moment, lift a glass of wine to Charlie and Uncle Steve!

21015 Geyserville Avenue | Geyserville, CA 95441
707-857-9870
mercurywine.com

BRAD'S DRY-RUB RIBS

Pair with The Rocket 6-year barrel-aged Red Blend

SERVES 8

2 tablespoons Lawry's seasoned salt

½ tablespoon ground black pepper

½ tablespoon onion powder

1 teaspoon granulated garlic

1 teaspoon cayenne pepper, or to taste

2 racks baby back pork ribs

1 liter Heinz white vinegar, in a spray bottle (use this brand for best flavor)

Combine all the dry ingredients in a bowl.

Place the ribs on a cookie sheet or pan large enough to hold them. Rub the ribs on both sides with the seasoning mixture. Cover the pan with foil and refrigerate the ribs for 6-12 hours before you cook them.

Preheat a grill to 215°-250°. Just before you place the ribs onto the grill, lightly spritz both sides of the meat with the white Heinz vinegar, being careful not to wash off the rub.

Place the ribs, meaty side up, on the grill. Close the lid and cook the ribs for 10-15 minutes. Watch for hot spots and use a spray bottle with water to take care of flare-ups. Open the grill lid, spray the ribs again with vinegar, flip them over and spray other side. Close the lid and cook the ribs another 10-15 minutes.

Continue this process for approximately 2 hours; you want to see the meat pulling from the bone a bit, and the ribs should be beginning to turn a crispy golden brown. Continue to spritz the ribs with vinegar every 10-15 minutes. At the 3-hour mark, focus on obtaining the golden brown color. If any parts of the ribs aren't yet brown, move them to a hotter spot on the grill and brown them for the last hour or so.

After 4 hours the ribs will be golden brown, crispy and falling-off-the-bone tender.

MERRIAM VINEYARDS

Chefs Duskie Estes and John Stewart are masters at butchering and cooking meat. In their inspired version of shepherd's pie, they incorporate both beef and pork – double the flavor in a dish that feeds a crowd. Top the slow-roasted meat with your favorite mashed potatoes.

11650 Los Amigos Road | Healdsburg, CA 95448
707-433-4032
merriamvineyards.com

ZAZU
SHORT RIB SHEPHERD'S PIE

Pair with Merriam Cabernet Sauvignon

SERVES 30

5 pounds bone-in beef short ribs

5 pounds bone-in pork shoulder

½ cup pure olive oil

4 quarts mirepoix (diced onion, carrot and celery)

1 bottle Merriam red wine

1 #10 can (12 cups) tomatoes

2-½ quarts chicken stock

1 bunch oregano, chopped

4 bay leaves

1 tablespoon Calabrian chili oil

1 teaspoon red pepper flakes

12 cloves garlic, peeled and smashed

kosher salt, to taste

freshly ground black pepper, to taste

mashed potatoes

Parmesan cheese, grated

2 cups gremolata (minced garlic, parsley, lemon zest)

Preheat oven to 350°.

Season the beef ribs and pork generously with salt. Add the oil to a heavy-bottom pan and sear the meat on high heat, until the beef and pork are browned on all sides. Set the meat aside.

Brown the diced carrots, celery and onion in the same pan. Add the meat back to the pan and pour in the wine. Simmer the meat for 5 minutes. Add the tomatoes, stock, oregano, bay leaves, chili oil, red pepper flakes, garlic, salt and black pepper, and enough water to cover the meat halfway. Cover the pan with foil and roast the meat until it's tender, 3-plus hours.

Increase oven temperature to 400°.

Remove the bones and bay leaves from the pan. Using tongs, place the meat in heat-proof serving bowls and top each bowl with a spoonful of mashed potatoes and a sprinkling of Parmesan cheese. Place the bowls in the oven until the potatoes are golden brown. Sprinkle the tops with gremolata and serve.

MUELLER WINERY

We can always count on Shari Sarabi to come up with something new and creative. This dish, which features funghi from Gourmet Mushrooms in Sebastopol, is simply delicious and highlights the complementary mushroom and Pinot Noir flavors. Gourmet Mushrooms' Nebrodini Bianco, Alba Clamshell, Brown Clamshell and Trumpet Royal are great choices. Serve them over creamy polenta.

118 North Street | Healdsburg, CA 95448
707-473-8086
muellerwine.com

GOURMET MUSHROOM RAGU
OVER CREAMY POLENTA

Pair with Mueller Emily's Cuvée Russian River Valley Pinot Noir

SERVES 6

MUSHROOMS

1 pound mixed Gourmet Mushrooms

2 tablespoons extra virgin olive oil

1 small sweet onion, finely chopped

2 cloves garlic, peeled and minced

2 ounces tomato paste

1 bay leaf

1 cup Mueller Emily's Cuvée
   Pinot Noir

1 cup rich veal stock

3 ounces sweet butter

¼ bunch fresh thyme, chopped

½ bunch Italian parsley, chopped

salt

freshly ground black pepper

POLENTA

1 tablespoon olive oil

1 medium yellow onion, finely diced

1 tablespoon garlic, minced

1 teaspoon rosemary

3 cups chicken stock

1 cup heavy cream

½ cup polenta

¼ pound butter

½ cup Parmesan cheese, grated

Trim the mushrooms and slice the large caps into fairly even pieces; leave the smaller caps intact.

Heat the oil in a large skillet over medium heat and sauté the mushrooms until they're tender. Add the onions and garlic and continue to cook until the onions are tender.

Add the tomato paste and bay leaf and mix well. Cook for another 2-3 minutes and deglaze the pan with the Pinot Noir. Sauté the mixture until the alcohol is evaporated, add the veal stock, and cook until the ragu is reduced to a sauce consistency.

Turn the heat off and add the butter, thyme and parsley. Stir to combine, and season to taste with salt and pepper. Keep the ragu warm while the polenta cooks.

To prepare the polenta, heat the oil in a large sauté pan. Add the onion, garlic and rosemary, and cook until the onions are translucent. Add 1 cup of the chicken stock and the cream, and bring the mixture to a boil. Reduce the heat and add the polenta, whisking until it's smooth. On low heat, cook the polenta for 30 minutes, frequently but slowly adding the remaining chicken stock so that the polenta does not get thick.

Remove the polenta from the heat and add the butter and Parmesan cheese while whisking. Spoon it over the mushrooms and top with grated Parmesan.

MURPHY GOODE WINERY

The trick to making good gumbo is to cook it low and slow – the flavor keeps improving with time. We like to serve this gumbo with Murphy-Goode Zinfandel, as the spices in the dish pair wonderfully with this rich, luscious wine.

20 Matheson Street | Healdsburg, CA 95448
800-499-7644
murphygoodewinery.com

REALLY GOODE GUMBO

Pair with Murphy Goode Liar's Dice Zinfandel

SERVES 6-8

1 cup vegetable oil

2 cups flour

2 cups onion, ½-inch dice

1 cup celery, ½-inch dice

1 cup green bell peppers,
½-inch dice

4 cloves garlic, minced

1 pound Andouille sausage,
½-inch dice

4 boneless chicken thighs,
½-inch dice

1 12-ounce can diced tomatoes

1-½ quarts chicken stock

1-½ quarts clam juice or crab stock

1 tablespoon Worcestershire sauce

1 tablespoon Tabasco sauce

1 tablespoon paprika

1 tablespoon garlic powder

1 tablespoon onion powder

1 tablespoon oregano

½ teaspoon cayenne pepper

½ teaspoon celery seed

1 teaspoon freshly ground black
pepper

2 cups okra, sliced

2 tablespoons filé powder

2 pounds shrimp, diced

1 pound Dungeness crab meat

kosher salt, to taste

In a large heavy-bottomed pot, heat the oil over medium-low heat. Add the flour and continue to stir until the roux turns very dark brown, approximately 30 minutes.

Add the onions, celery, bell peppers and garlic and cook for 10 minutes. Add the sausage and chicken; cook for 5 minutes. Add the tomatoes, chicken stock, clam juice, Worcestershire and Tabasco sauce and the remaining spices, except for the filé powder. Cook for at least 1 hour, until the mixture is thick.

Skim the fat and any impurities that rise to the top. The gumbo will get better the longer it is cooked. Be sure to stir and cook slowly over very low heat.

Add the okra and filé powder. Cook the gumbo for 5 minutes, then add the shrimp and crab. Cook for 5 minutes more and season with salt to taste. Serve the gumbo over white rice.

OLD WORLD WINERY

Winemaker Darek Trowbridge and chef Helena Giesea are happy to be working together again, as they have done for many winemaker dinners. Darek is known for producing wines from unusual grape varieties, and Helena is known for her creative use of wild game and other non-mainstream meats. They've challenged each other for Wine & Food Affair; check out the results!

850 River Road | Fulton, CA 95439
707-490-6696
oldworldwinery.com

BISON MEATBALLS
WITH WARM CHERRY-MUSHROOM RICE SALAD

Pair with Abourious Russian River Red

SERVES 4

RICE SALAD

2 cups brown basmati rice
½ cup California wild rice
5 cups cold water
2 tablespoons dried mushrooms, crushed into dust
2 tablespoons carrot, diced fine
2 tablespoons celery, diced fine
2 tablespoons red onion, diced fine
1 teaspoon sea salt
¼ cup fresh goat cheese
¼ cup dried cherries
2 tablespoons orange rind, micro-grated
2 cups orange juice, room temperature
½ cup Abourious wine
2 tablespoons honey

MEATBALLS

2 eggs
½ cup whole milk
1 cup plain bread crumbs
1 pound grass-fed bison, ground
1 teaspoon Dijon mustard
1 tablespoon onion powder
¼ teaspoon nutmeg
1 tablespoon paprika
2 pinches cayenne pepper
1 tablespoon black pepper
2-½ teaspoons sea salt

To begin the rice salad, place in a pot both rices, cold water, mushroom dust, carrot, celery, onion and salt. Bring the mixture to a boil and simmer it for approximately 40 minutes, or until the water has evaporated and the rice is fully cooked.

While the rice cooks, prepare the meatballs by first preheating the oven to 375°.

Whip the eggs in a mixing bowl and add the milk. Soak the bread crumbs in the egg mixture, then add the rest of ingredients to the bowl and mix well.

Roll the meat mixture into 1 to 1-½ ounce balls. Place the meatballs on a greased sheet pan and bake them for 20-30 minutes.

Scoop the rice into a large bowl and let it sit to cool a little. Fold in the cheese, cherries and orange rind into the warm rice. Bring the orange juice, wine and honey to a boil in a saucepan and simmer on low, until the liquid is reduced by ½.

Pour the sauce over the rice and season with salt and pepper. Serve 5-6 meatballs over the warm salad.

PAPAPIETRO PERRY

When our assistant winemaker, Dave Low, got married last year, this amuse bouche was served at his wedding as a surprise gift from the chef. When it came time to decide on something special to share for Wine & Food Affair, this dish was an obvious choice. Chef Bruce Riezenman follows the tradition of using milk in Bolognese: "It adds a background sweetness and richness that combines wonderfully with earthy mushrooms and Pinot Noir." We serve this wonderful sauce over cavatappi pasta.

4791 Dry Creek Road #4 | Healdsburg, CA 95448
707-433-0422
papapietro-perry.com

WILD BOAR BOLOGNESE

Pair with Papapietro Perry Russian River Valley Pinot Noir

SERVES 6

3 tablespoons butter

2 ounces (by weight) raw pancetta, minced

2 tablespoons celery, fine dice

2 tablespoons carrot, fine dice

2 tablespoons yellow onion, fine dice

salt and pepper, to taste

¾ pound ground wild boar, medium grind

½ cup milk

1 cup Papapietro Perry Pinot Noir

6 ounces diced tomatoes in juice, chopped fine (save juice)

6 sprigs fresh thyme

1 teaspoon ground juniper berries

4 each large sage leaves

2 tablespoons dried porcini powder

2 tablespoons dried porcini mushrooms

¼ teaspoon red pepper flakes

½ cup veal or beef broth

In a sauté pan, heat the butter and pancetta and cook until the pancetta is slightly crisped. Add the celery, carrot and onion, plus some salt and pepper. Cook, covered, over medium heat until the vegetables soften but are not browned. Add the ground boar and a little more salt, and "crumble" the meat by mashing it with the back of a spoon.

Continue to cook until the meat has changed color but has not yet browned. Add the milk and simmer until it has evaporated and only clear fat remains. Add the Pinot Noir and simmer the mixture until the wine has evaporated. Add the tomatoes, thyme, juniper berries, sage, porcini powder and mushrooms, red pepper flakes and broth.

Bring the Bolognese to a simmer, then reduce the heat to the lowest possible simmer. Cook the sauce at a slight bubble for an additional 2 hours. Adjust the seasoning with salt and pepper, and serve.

PAUL MATHEW VINEYARDS

We're former sommeliers (Mat and Barb Gustafson) and often have several bottles of wine open when we dine at home, to test various pairings. We adore curry and make it at least once a week. We wanted to share a recipe that is easy to make and goes great with our wine. Most people would not think of matching Pinot Noir with curry, but it's great!

9060 Graton Road | Graton, CA 95444
707-861-9729
paulmathewvineyards.com

CHICKEN CURRY STEW

Pair with Paul Mathew Russian River Valley Pinot Noir

SERVES 6-8

2 tablespoons butter

1 whole chicken, cut into
   12 pieces

2 medium red onions

4 tablespoons butter

7 cloves garlic

3 cups chicken broth

3 cups water

2 large sweet potatoes, peeled
   and cut into ½-inch cubes

2 red peppers, medium dice

1 tablespoon Vindaloo curry
   powder

salt and pepper, to taste

1 bunch Thai basil, chopped

juice of 2 limes

Melt the butter in a heavy frying pan and brown the chicken pieces, skin side first. Set the chicken aside.

Dice 1 onion, smash 3 garlic cloves, and add them to a stock pot. Add the chicken broth and water. Add the browned chicken and bring the contents to a simmer. Cook until the chicken is tender, about 40 minutes, then remove the pieces from the pot and let them cool. Continue to simmer the stock and vegetables.

Remove the skin and bones from the chicken and add them to the stock. Cut the chicken meat into bite-size pieces and set them aside. Cook the stock for as long as possible and reduce it down to 5 cups. Strain the stock and remove the fat.

Melt 2 tablespoons of butter in a heavy saucepan and add the remaining onion, medium dice, and cook for 2 minutes on medium-high. Cut the remaining 4 garlic cloves into small dice, add them to the pan, and continue to sauté for 3 more minutes. Add the 5 cups of chicken stock, sweet potato cubes, red peppers and curry powder.

Cook the mixture until the potatoes are soft, 15-20 minutes. Add the chicken pieces and season with salt and pepper. When the chicken is warmed through, add the Thai basil and lime juice, and serve.

PECH MERLE WINERY

This has become our "go-to" dish for dinner with family and friends. Everyone seriously loves it! We serve the pot roast over creamy polenta and with a side of roasted root vegetables.

24505 Chianti Road | Cloverdale, CA 95425
707-585-9599
pechmerlewinery.com

PERFECT SUNDAY POT ROAST
WITH RICH CABERNET GRAVY

Pair with Pech Merle Alexander Valley Cabernet Sauvignon

SERVES 5-6

1 boneless chuck roast,
  3-½ pounds

1 tablespoon dried rosemary

1-½ teaspoons dried basil

1 teaspoon kosher salt

½ teaspoon freshly ground
  black pepper

½ teaspoon red pepper flakes

3 tablespoons olive oil

1-½ cups onions, finely diced

1 cup carrot, finely diced

¾ cup celery, finely diced

3 large garlic cloves, crushed
  and peeled

3 bay leaves, broken in ½

1 28-ounce can diced tomatoes,
  drained

3 cups beef broth

2 cups Pech Merle Cabernet
  Sauvignon

½ cup orange juice

2 tablespoons Italian parsley,
  chopped

Preheat oven to 275°.

Pat the roast dry with paper towels. In a small bowl, combine the rosemary, basil, salt, black pepper and red pepper flakes. Rub the mixture on all sides of the roast.

In a deep-sided oven-proof pot with a lid, heat 2 tablespoons of the oil over medium heat. Add the roast and brown it on all sides, about 5 minutes. Set the meat aside.

In the same pot, heat the remaining 1 tablespoon of oil and add the onions, carrots and celery. Cook until they're softened, about 3-5 minutes. Add the garlic and sauté for 1 minute. Add the bay leaves, tomatoes, broth, wine and orange juice. Bring the mixture to a simmer, return the meat to the pot, cover it and roast it in the oven until it's fork tender, about 2-½ hours.

Remove the roast to a serving platter. Discard the bay leaves, and skim off any fat that has accumulated. Puree the warm vegetable/liquid mixture – this is the rich gravy.

To serve, slice the roast ¼-inch thick and sprinkle it with the parsley. Serve the meat with the gravy.

PORTALUPI WINE

The Portalupi family hails from a small village in the Piemonte region of Northern Italy. It is there that Marina Portalupi began honing her cooking skills, which she passed down to all of us. Our recipes are inspired by the great Italian food we grew up with, prepared by our matriarch, Marina.

107 North Street | Healdsburg, CA 95448
707-395-0960
portalupiwine.com

POLPETTE E POLENTA
(MEATBALLS WITH POLENTA)

Pair with Portalupi Russian River Valley Old Vine Zinfandel

SERVES 8

POLENTA

2 cups cornmeal
2 cups cold water
2 teaspoons salt
3 cups boiling water
2 cups Parmesan cheese, grated
½ to 1 cup olive oil

MEATBALLS

1 pound ground beef
½ pound ground veal
½ pound Italian ground pork
2 cloves garlic, minced
2 eggs
1 cup Pecorino Romano cheese, grated
1-½ tablespoons Italian parsley, chopped
1-½ tablespoon fresh oregano, chopped
salt and ground black pepper, to taste
2 cups Italian bread crumbs

SAUCE

2 14.5-ounce cans stewed tomatoes
1 6-ounce can tomato paste
4 tablespoons parsley, minced
1 clove garlic, minced
1 tablespoon fresh oregano, minced
1 teaspoon salt
1 teaspoon ground black pepper
6 tablespoons olive oil
⅓ cup onion, finely diced
½ cup Portalupi Bianco white wine
Parmesan cheese, for garnish
parsley sprigs, for garnish

First prepare the polenta by combining the cornmeal, cold water and salt in a mixing bowl. Grease a large baking dish. In a large saucepan, bring 3 cups of water to a boil. Stir in the cornmeal mixture and return the pan to a boil, stirring constantly. Reduce the heat to a simmer, and stir in the cheese. Let the mixture simmer for 20 minutes, stirring frequently, until it's thick. Spread the mixture into the prepared baking dish and place it in the refrigerator for 4 hours or overnight.

To prepare the meatballs, preheat oven to 400°.

Combine the beef, veal and pork in a large bowl. Add the garlic, eggs, cheese, parsley, oregano, salt and pepper. Blend the bread crumbs into the meat. Shape the mixture into 1-inch meatballs. Place them on an oiled cookie sheet and bake for 15-20 minutes. Roll the meatballs halfway through the cooking time so that they bake evenly.

To prepare the sauce, place the tomatoes, tomato paste, parsley, garlic, oregano, salt and pepper in a food processor. Blend until smooth. In a large skillet over medium heat, sauté the onion in the olive oil for 2 minutes. Add the pureed tomato sauce and white wine. Simmer the sauce for 30 minutes, stirring occasionally.

Ten minutes before you are ready to serve the dish, cut the refrigerated polenta into squares. Heat the olive oil in a pan and fry the squares on both sides, about 3 minutes each.

Place 2-3 fried polenta squares on a plate with a meatball on each, and spoon over the sauce. Garnish with shredded Parmesan and parsley sprigs.

RAMAZZOTTI WINES

Prepare this dish when you're in the mood to "spice" things up a bit! It's a Southern-roots gumbo and is superb with our deep, intense Ricordo ("remembrance" in Italian) Zinfandel-based field-blend wine.

21015 Geyserville Avenue | Geyserville, CA 95441
707-814-0016
ramazzottiwines.com

SWEET T'S GUMBO

Pair with Ramazzotti Ricordo Zinfandel Field Blend

SERVES 8

SEASONING

2-½ tablespoons paprika

2 tablespoons salt

2 tablespoons garlic powder

1 tablespoon black pepper

1 tablespoon onion powder

1 tablespoon cayenne pepper

1 tablespoon dried oregano

1 tablespoon dried thyme

GUMBO

1 tablespoon plus 1 cup canola oil

1 pound Andouille sausage, cut
    crosswise into ½-inch-thick pieces

1 cup all purpose flour

2 cups onions, chopped

1 cup celery, chopped

1 cup green bell peppers, chopped

1 tablespoon gumbo seasoning

1 cup okra, cleaned and sliced

1 teaspoon salt

¼ teaspoon cayenne pepper

3 bay leaves

9 cups chicken stock/broth

4 pounds smoked chicken,
    pulled and skin removed

½ cup green onions, chopped

2 tablespoons parsley leaves, chopped

1 tablespoon filé powder

white rice

Tabasco pepper sauce

Prepare the gumbo seasoning by combining all the ingredients in a small bowl. Mix thoroughly, and set it aside.

To prepare the gumbo, heat 1 tablespoon of the canola oil in a large sauté pan over medium-high heat. Add the sausage and cook until it's well browned, about 8 minutes. Remove the sausage with a slotted spoon and allow it to drain on paper towels.

Combine the remaining 1 cup of oil and the flour in the same pan over medium heat and cook, stirring continuously to prevent burning. The flour will begin to change color from white, to tan, to orange, to red, to light brown, to dark brown. Medium to dark brown is the color you want. This takes about 15-20 minutes.

Add the onions, celery and bell peppers and cook, stirring, until the onions are translucent, 4-5 minutes. Add the cooked Andouille sausage, okra, gumbo seasoning salt, cayenne and bay leaves, stir, and cook the mixture for 2 minutes. Slowly add the chicken stock, stirring constantly, and continue to cook until the mixture is combined and reaches a simmering boil.

Reduce the heat to medium-low and cook the gumbo uncovered, stirring occasionally, for 1 hour, skimming off any fat that rises to the surface. You are looking for a consistency that is thicker than soup but not as thick as stew. Add more or less chicken broth to achieve this.

Remove the pot from the heat. Using a slotted spoon, remove the bay leaves. Add the smoked chicken, green onions, parsley and filé powder and stir to combine.

To serve, spoon steamed white rice into deep bowls and ladle the gumbo on top. Serve with the Tabasco pepper sauce on the side.

ROADHOUSE WINERY

"Pigs and Pinot" work well together, and you are in for a real treat with this pairing. We love this dish on those cool fall nights when we can find time away from the hustle and bustle of harvest to enjoy food and wine with friends.

240 Center Street | Healdsburg, CA 95448
707-922-6362
roadhousewinery.com

BRAISED PORK
WITH HERBED POLENTA

Pair with Roadhouse Russian River Valley Pinot Noir

SERVES 6 8

PORK

6 pounds boneless pork butt

½ cup kosher salt

1 tablespoon black pepper

1 pound yellow onions, quartered

⅔ pound jumbo carrots, rough cut

¼ bunch celery, washed and rough cut

1.5 ounces garlic, peeled

½ ounce chile de arbol dried pepper

2 cups water

2 tablespoons red wine vinegar

salt and pepper

POLENTA

9 cups water

1 tablespoon salt, plus extra for seasoning

2-½ cups yellow cornmeal

1-½ cups Parmesan cheese, grated

1-½ cups whole milk

1-¼ sticks unsalted butter, room temperature

⅓ cup flat leaf parsley, chopped

freshly ground white pepper

Preheat oven to 350°.

Rub the pork liberally with salt and pepper. In a wide, heavy-bottom pot, sear the meat on both sides over medium-high heat.

Drain the fat from the pot and add the onions, carrots, celery, garlic and chile de arbol. Sear the vegetables until they start to turn golden, about 10 minutes. Place the seared pork, vegetables and the water in a 6-inch-deep pan and cover it with foil. Place the pan in the preheated oven for 3 hours.

Let the pork and vegetables cool for 30 minutes. Use a fork to pull apart the meat. Transfer the vegetables and drippings to a blender and puree them to make the sauce; add the vinegar and salt and pepper, to taste.

While the pork cools, prepare the herbed polenta. Bring the water to a boil in a large pot. Add the salt. Gradually whisk in the cornmeal. Reduce the heat to low and cook, stirring often, until the mixture thickens and the cornmeal is tender, 15-20 minutes.

Remove the polenta from the heat and add the cheese, milk and butter, stirring until the butter and cheese have melted. Add the parsley and season with salt and white pepper.

Place the polenta in a large, wide serving bowl and top it with the pork; drizzle the sauce on top of the meat. Garnish with Parmesan and fresh parsley, if desired.

RUED VINEYARDS

This twist on a classic cottage pie features a hearty filling of ground beef, salty olives, savory tomatoes and warming spices, which rein in the sweetness of the creamy sweet potato topping. It's a perfect dish for a crisp autumn evening in Sonoma County.

3850 Dry Creek Road | Healdsburg, CA 95448
707-433-3261
ruedvineyards.com

SWEET POTATO COTTAGE PIE

Pair with Rued Vineyards Dry Creek Valley Zinfandel

SERVES 4-6

TOPPING

2 large sweet potatoes

½ cup whole milk

¼ cup Parmesan cheese, grated

2 tablespoons unsalted butter, softened

1 teaspoon kosher salt

½ teaspoon freshly ground black pepper

FILLING

2 tablespoons olive oil

2 celery ribs, ¼-inch dice

1 large carrot, ¼ inch dice

1 medium onion, finely chopped

kosher salt

3 medium cloves garlic, minced

2 teaspoons ground cumin

2 teaspoons chopped fresh oregano or ½ teaspoon dried oregano

1 teaspoon chili powder

¾ teaspoon ground cinnamon

1-½ pounds ground beef

1 14-ounce can whole, peeled tomatoes

½ cup pimento-stuffed green olives, coarsely chopped

½ cup raisins or dried cranberries, coarsely chopped

Preheat oven to 425°.

To prepare the topping, position the rack in the center of the preheated oven. Line a heavy-duty rimmed baking sheet with foil.

Slice the sweet potatoes in ½ lengthwise and set them, cut side down, on the baking sheet. Roast the potatoes until they're very tender, about 30 minutes.

When the sweet potatoes are cool enough to handle, scoop their flesh into a medium bowl. Add the milk, cheese, butter, salt and pepper, and beat with a hand mixer on low speed until the mixture is smooth and creamy, about 1 minute. Set it aside.

Lower the oven temperature to 350°.

Prepare the filling by heating the oil in a 12-inch sauté pan over medium-high heat. Add the celery, carrots, onion and 1 teaspoon of salt. Reduce the heat to medium and cook, stirring frequently, until the vegetables are soft, about 10-15 minutes. Add the garlic, cumin, oregano, chili powder and cinnamon and cook for 30 seconds. Add the beef, season with 2 teaspoons of salt and cook the meat until it is no longer pink, about 5 minutes. Tilt the pan and spoon off all but 1 tablespoon of the fat, and return the pan to the heat.

Pour the tomatoes and their juice into a small bowl and crush them with your hands or a fork. Add the tomatoes to the meat mixture and cook, uncovered, until the mixture is thick, 10-12 minutes. Add the olives and the raisins/dried cranberries and cook for another few minutes. Season to taste with salt.

Transfer the beef mixture to a 9-inch by 9-inch baking dish. Spread the sweet potatoes over the top in an even layer. Bake for about 30 minutes, until the pie is bubbling around the edges. Let it cool for at least 15 minutes before serving.

SELBY WINERY

The inspiration for this dish came from a trip to France. Taureau de Camargue is the region of origin for the most famous beef in the world. Although Zinfandel is not indigenous to France, the visit had me thinking about a recipe that incorporates Bobcat Zinfandel. After multiple trials, the conclusion was that the wine is the most important ingredient – and high-quality beef, of course. The sacrifice of a bottle of Bobcat is well worth it for this recipe!

215 Center Street | Healdsburg, CA 95448
707-431-1288
selbywinery.com

LE BOEUF DE BOBCAT

Pair with Selby Zinfandel

SERVES 6

3-½ pounds chuck roast, boneless

salt and ground black pepper

4 ounces pancetta, cut into ¼-inch cubes

2 medium onions, chopped

2 medium carrots, chopped

2 ribs celery, chopped

1 tablespoon tomato paste

3 cloves garlic, minced

1 bottle Selby Bobcat Zinfandel

1 14-½ ounce can diced tomatoes, drained

1 tablespoon fresh oregano, chopped

1 teaspoon fresh rosemary, minced

If your roast is very fatty, trim some of the fat – but be sure to leave enough to keep the meat moist during braising. Salt and pepper the roast well and let it sit at room temperature while you prepare the vegetables.

Pour a splash of water into a Dutch oven. Place it over medium heat and add the pancetta. As soon as the water begins to simmer, lower the heat to medium-low and slowly crisp the pancetta to a golden brown color. Remove it with a slotted spoon and set it aside.

Preheat oven to 300°.

Pat the beef roast dry with a paper towel. Increase the heat to medium under the Dutch oven and place the roast in it. Brown the meat on all sides. Transfer the roast to a bowl, and add the onions, carrot and celery to the Dutch oven. Sprinkle salt over the vegetables while they cook. Increase the heat to medium-high and sauté for 2-3 minutes.

Add the tomato paste, stir well, and sauté for another 1-2 minutes. Add the garlic and cook 1 minute more. Increase the heat to high and add the Zinfandel, tomatoes, oregano, rosemary and cooked pancetta. Nestle the roast in the Dutch oven, cover it with the lid, and cook it for 3 hours in the oven. At the halfway point, use tongs to turn over the roast.

Transfer the roast to a large bowl and tent it with foil to keep it warm. Allow the liquid to settle in the Dutch oven for a few minutes. Skim off the fat with a wide, shallow spoon. Use an immersion blender to blend the contents of the pot. Boil the sauce until it is reduced to 3-½ cups. Strain the liquid through a large fine-mesh strainer, pressing on the solids with a spatula to extract as much liquid as possible. Boil the sauce again until it has reduced to 1-½ cups. Season the sauce with salt and pepper.

Cut the meat into ½-inch-thick slices and pour the sauce over them. Serve with mashed potatoes or crusty bread.

SKEWIS WINES

Pissaladière – classic Provencal pizza — calls for whole anchovies, though we eliminated them from this recipe because their salt tends to drop away the fruit in our Pinot Noir. Instead, we add a touch of mozzarella for richness.

57 Front Street | Healdsburg, CA 95448
707-431-2160
skewiswines.com

VEGI

PISSALADIÈRE SKEWIS STYLE

Pair with Skewis Peters Vineyard Pinot Noir

SERVES 6

DOUGH

¼ ounce active dry yeast

1 cup warm water

¼ cup extra virgin olive oil

3 cups flour

1 tablespoon sea salt

cornmeal, for dusting

TOPPING

2 sprigs thyme

2 springs marjoram

1 sprig rosemary

¼ cup extra virgin olive oil

2-3 pounds onions, peeled and
   thinly sliced

salt

freshly ground black pepper

⅓ cup pitted niçoise olives

¼ cup mozzarella cheese, grated

Prepare the dough by dissolving the yeast in warm water in a small bowl. Let it stand for 5 minutes, then add the oil. Combine the flour and salt in a medium bowl, add the yeast mixture, and stir with a wooden spoon, adding a bit more water if necessary, until ingredients are well mixed.

Turn out the dough on a lightly floured work surface and dust your hands with flour. Knead the dough for several minutes, until it has a smooth, firm, elastic character. Form the dough into a ball and place it in a lightly oiled bowl. Cover the dough with a damp cloth and allow it to rise in a warm spot for about 1 hour.

To prepare the topping, make a bouquet garni by tying the thyme, marjoram and rosemary sprigs together with kitchen twine. Heat the oil in a large skillet over medium heat. Add the onions and season them generously with salt and pepper. Add the bouquet garni and cover the pan. Simmer the onions slowly for 45 minutes over medium heat, stirring occasionally. Be very careful not to burn them. Uncover the pan and continue cooking until the moisture has evaporated and the onions are very tender and have marmalade-like consistency, 30-40 minutes. Drain the onions in a colander to remove any excess oil.

On a floured surface, roll the dough into a thin, flat rectangle. Transfer it to an 11-inch by 17-inch baking sheet dusted with cornmeal. Cover the dough with a damp cloth and allow it to rest for 30 minutes.

Preheat oven to 375°.

Remove the cloth from the dough and spread the onion mixture on top. Pat the oil and liquid from the olives by placing them between paper towels. Arrange the olives over the onions and season lightly with pepper. Bake the pizza until the crust has browned, 15-20 minutes. Serve warm or at room temperature, cut into wedges.

SODA ROCK WINERY

This is a dish that our winemaker — and my mother, Diane — made for our family after I graduated from university. I had been a vegetarian for four years, and this was the first meal to entice me back into the world of carnivorism. It has become a family favorite, and a recipe requested by friends far and wide.
- *Victoria Wilson*

8015 Highway 128 | Healdsburg, CA 95448
707-433-3303
sodarockwinery.com

SODA ROCKIN' PORK CHILE VERDE

Pair with Soda Rock Primitivo

SERVES 12

½ cup extra virgin olive oil

5 cups onions, chopped

10 cloves garlic, minced

5 jalapeno peppers, diced

5 pounds pork shoulder, cubed

2 cups Soda Rock Chardonnay

1 quart chicken stock

15 mild Anaheim peppers

25 tomatillos, papery skins removed

2 cloves garlic, minced

1 teaspoon freshly ground black pepper

1 tablespoon ground cumin

1 tablespoon fresh or dried oregano

1 teaspoon ground coriander

2 teaspoons salt

Preheat oven to 350°.

In a medium saucepan, add the olive oil, onion, garlic and jalapenos and cook over medium heat until the onions are tender, about 5 minutes. Remove the pan from the heat.

Place the pork in a large, heavy-bottomed pot coated with oil. Turn the heat to medium and sear the meat until it's browned on all sides. Add the Chardonnay and cook until the liquid is reduced by ½. Add the chicken stock and the onion mixture. Turn the heat to low and simmer the mixture.

Place the Anaheim peppers and tomatillos on a sheet pan. Coat them with olive oil and roast them in the oven until the peppers are slightly charred and the tomatillos are soft, about 20 minutes. Remove the pan from the oven and place the peppers in a plastic bag. Let them steam for 5 minutes.

Peel and seed the peppers, then blend them with the tomatillos in a food processor. Add the puree to the simmering pork mixture, stir, and continue simmering on low heat.

Combine the garlic, black pepper, cumin, oregano, coriander and salt in a small bowl, then add it to pork mixture. Stir well. Simmer the pork for 1-½-2 hours on medium-low heat, or until the pork is fork-tender. Serve the chile verde over rice.

STARLITE VINEYARDS

Applewood-smoked sea salt adds a rich, smoky aroma and flavor to these lamb skewers. You can find it in gourmet grocery stores and online — Amazon sells it, for example. If you have access to a smoker, you can smoke your own salt; applewood is the preferred wood.

5511 Highway 128 | Geyserville, CA 95441
707-431-1102
starlitevineyards.com

MEDITERRANEAN LAMB SPEAR

Pair with Starlite Vineyards Zinfandel

SERVES 12

3 pounds lamb top round

applewood-smoked sea salt, to taste

salt and pepper, to taste

1-⅓ cups extra virgin olive oil

½ cup almonds, toasted

1 bunch wild arugula

1 bunch of Greek basil

juice 1 lemon

4 garlic cloves, peeled

2 fennel bulbs, cored and thinly sliced (save tops for garnish)

36 bamboo skewers

Preheat a grill to medium-high.

Season the lamb with the smoked sea salt, black pepper and ⅓ cup of the olive oil. Grill the meat to the desired doneness; rare is recommended. Let the cooked lamb rest while you prepare the pesto and fennel.

Place the toasted almonds in a food processor and chop them coarsely. Add ⅔ cup olive oil and the arugula, basil, lemon, and garlic, and puree until the pesto is creamy. Season with salt and pepper.

To prepare the fennel, place the remaining ⅓ cup olive oil in a sauté pan and warm it over low heat. Add the fennel slices and cook them until they're caramelized.

To assemble the skewers, cut the lamb into 1-ounce slices. On each skewer, thread a slice of lamb, place 1 tablespoon of pesto on top of the meat, and add 1 tablespoon of caramelized fennel. Garnish with the fennel tops.

STONESTREET WINERY

Don't wait for the cold of winter to make this hearty dish. This rich and flavorful stew is simple to prepare and best served at the table with family, friends and a glass of Cabernet Sauvignon.

7111 Highway 128 | Healdsburg, CA 95448
800-355-8008
stonestreetwines.com

PEARL BARLEY & BEEF STEW

Pair with Stonestreet Bear Point Cabernet Sauvignon

SERVES 8

1 cup dried pearl barley

3 pounds lean boneless beef chuck, cut into 2-inch pieces

kosher salt

freshly ground black pepper

3 tablespoons olive oil

1 carrot, quartered

2 celery stalks, cut into quarters

1 onion, quartered

1 head of garlic, cut in ½ crosswise

¼ cup tomato paste

1 bay leaf

1 star anise

1 small cinnamon stick

1 tablespoon dried thyme

2-½ cups dry red wine

3 cups beef broth

1-½ cups water

2 parsnips, peeled, halved and cut on a bias ½-inch thick

1 small rutabaga, peeled and cut into wedges ½-inch thick

Preheat oven to 300°.

In a medium bowl, add the barley and cover it with cold water. Set aside.

Heat an 8-quart pot over medium-high heat. Pat the beef dry and season it generously with salt and pepper. Add the oil to the pan and brown the meat on all sides; do this in 2-3 batches to ensure even browning. Transfer the cooked meat to a bowl.

Reduce the heat to medium. Add to the pot the carrot, celery, onion and garlic, and cook until the vegetables are well roasted, approximately 12-15 minutes. Add the tomato paste and cook, stirring constantly, for 2 minutes. Add the bay leaf, star anise, cinnamon stick, thyme and a pinch of salt. Add the wine and cook until the liquid is reduced by ½. Add to the braising pot the broth, water, meat and its juices. Bring to a simmer and skim off any foam that collects on the surface. Cover the pot and place it in the oven for 1 hour, or until the meat is very tender.

Remove the pot from the oven but don't turn off the heat. Use a ladle to remove the fat from the braising liquid. Drain and rinse the barley. Add the barley, parsnips and rutabaga to the pot and bring the stew to a simmer on the stovetop. Place the pot back in the oven for 35 minutes. The stew is done when the barley is soft. Taste and adjust the seasonings if necessary.

SUNCE WINERY

This dish is one of Sunce's standbys. It wasn't easy getting the recipe from our in-house cook, Denise Stewart, but we used bribery and it worked! Her "Secret Sauce" is no longer a secret. We like to serve these sandwiches with a fruity Hawaiian-style cole slaw.

1839 Olivet Road | Santa Rosa, CA 95401
707-526-9463
suncewinery.com

DENISE'S FAMOUS
PULLED PORK SANDWICHES

Pair with Sunce Cattich Vineyard Russian River Valley Zinfandel

SERVES 6

PORK

1 yellow onion, sliced

½ teaspoon black pepper

½ teaspoon garlic granules

½ teaspoon seasoned salt

½ teaspoon chili powder

½ teaspoon cayenne pepper

1 4-pound pork roast

2 cups water or 2 bottles beer

6 sourdough buns

DENISE'S BBQ SAUCE

1 32-ounce bottle Heinz ketchup

1-½ cups apple cider vinegar

½ cup golden brown sugar

¼ cup Worcestershire sauce

2 tablespoons lemon juice

½ teaspoon horseradish

DENISE'S SECRET SAUCE

1 7-ounce can Herdez
    Salsa Verde

1 can Best Foods mayonnaise
    (measure with Herdez can)

½ can Heinz ketchup

1 tablespoon dark chili powder

To prepare the pork, coat the inside of a slow cooker with nonstick spray. Place the sliced onion at the bottom of the pot.

In a small bowl, mix all the dry seasonings together (black pepper through cayenne). Rub the mixture all over the roast. Place it on top of the onions in the slow cooker and add enough water or beer to fill the crock pot ⅔ full. Cover the pot and cook the meat on low for 8-12 hours or overnight.

Meanwhile, prepare the barbecue sauce by placing all the ingredients in a saucepan. Bring the mixture to a soft boil for 6 minutes. This can be done in advance and the sauce stored in the refrigerator until you're ready to use it.

Also prepare the "secret" sauce by mixing all the ingredients in a bowl. Transfer the sauce to a squeeze bottle and refrigerate.

Remove the roast from the slow cooker and discard the bone and fat, as well as any water, onions and grease remaining in the pot. When the meat is cool enough to handle, use a fork or your fingers to shred it. Return the pork to the crock pot. Mix in 16 ounces of the barbecue sauce, replace the lid, and cook on medium-high for 1-3 hours.

Serve the pulled pork on soft sourdough buns doused with Denise's Secret Sauce.

TOAD HOLLOW VINEYARDS

This is a twist on the classic pork carnitas taco, but with a clean, fresh taste. When I was growing up, my mother, Rosemary, would make carnitas for all my sporting fundraisers. After long hours at these events, it was great for my friends and family to have this warm and satisfying meal to fill our bellies! Sharing carnitas became a fun tradition.

409-A Healdsburg Avenue | Healdsburg, CA 95448
707-431-8667
toadhollow.com

WINTER CARNITAS TACOS

Pair with Toad Hollow Eye of the Toad Dry Rosé of Pinot Noir

SERVES 8

SALSA

1 yellow pepper, chopped coarse

1 onion, chopped coarse

1-½ tablespoons olive oil

juice and zest of 2 navel oranges

1 jalapeño, seeded and chopped

1 tablespoon canned chipotle
   chilies in adobo, minced

28 ounces whole canned Italian
   plum tomatoes, seeded and
   drained

1 green bell pepper, seeded and
   chopped

1 tablespoon cilantro, chopped

1 tablespoon fresh lime juice

PORK

4 pounds pork butt

4 tablespoons salt

4 tablespoons pepper

5 tablespoons cumin

2 tablespoons onion powder

1 tablespoon garlic salt

6 garlic cloves

2 cups Coco Rico coconut soda

2-½ cups chicken stock

1-½ cups Toad Hollow Dry Rosé
   of Pinot Noir

1 yellow onion, chopped into
   large chunks

Prepare the salsa by sautéing the pepper and onion in the olive oil over medium-high heat, until the vegetables are just tender and starting to turn brown. Grate the orange zest and set it aside. Add the orange juice, jalapeno and chipotle chiles to the onion mixture. Saute them for 1 minute. Pulse the tomatoes and orange zest in a food processor a few times, then add the onion mixture, green bell pepper, cilantro and lime juice. Puree into a salsa consistency. Transfer the salsa to a glass jar and refrigerate it until you're ready to serve the carnitas. It will last for 1 week.

Preheat oven to 400°.

Season the meat on all sides with salt and pepper. Place the pork in a large roasting pan. Mix the cumin, onion powder and garlic salt in a small bowl and pat the spice mixture all over the meat. Using a paring knife, cut 6 small pockets into the meat at various points and insert 1 garlic clove in each pocket.

Add the Coco Rico soda, stock, wine and onion chunks to the pan. Cover it with foil and bake the pork for 3 hours. Remove the foil, turn the meat over, and continue to cook it for 1 more hour. When the meat is tender, allow it to cool. Place it in a large bowl and pull the pork into small shreds with forks. Stir the pan juices into the shredded meat.

Serve the carnitas in warm tortillas and garnish with the salsa, crema Mexicana, radish slices, finely chopped onion, lime wedges and cilantro.

TRATTORE ESTATE WINES

We equate eating at Catelli's restaurant with enjoying a home-cooked meal in our own kitchen – yet without the work! Three generations of Catellis have made these meatballs, and they're among our family favorites.

4791 Dry Creek Road #9 | Healdsburg, CA 95448
707-431-7200
trattorewines.com

CATELLI'S MEATBALLS

Pair with Trattore Dry Creek Valley Zinfandel

SERVES 6-8

SAUCE

2 tablespoons Dry Creek Olive Co. extra virgin olive oil

4-5 cloves garlic cloves, ¼-inch pieces

½ teaspoon red pepper flakes

1 28-ounce can organic crushed tomatoes

½ teaspoon salt

MEATBALLS

1 pound ground beef

1 pound ground sausage (preferably pork and spicy)

½ cup onion, finely chopped

¼ cup garlic, minced

2 tablespoons fresh thyme, chopped

1 tablespoon fresh parsley, chopped, plus more for garnish

1 egg

½ cup Parmesan cheese, grated, plus more for garnish

1 cup panko bread crumbs

12 ounces ricotta cheese

2 tablespoons kosher salt

2 tablespoons Dry Creek Olive Co. extra virgin olive oil

To prepare the sauce, heat the olive oil in a large saucepan. Add the garlic and pepper flakes and sauté them over medium heat for 1 minute. Do not brown the garlic. Stir in the tomatoes and salt. Bring the sauce to a boil, reduce the heat to low, and simmer, stirring occasionally, for 15 minutes. Keep the sauce warm while you prepare the meatballs.

Preheat oven to 450°.

Mix together in a large bowl the beef, sausage, onions, garlic, thyme, parsley, egg, Parmesan, bread crumbs, ricotta and salt. Use your hands, like mixing Play-Doh. Form 1-½-inch balls out of the meat mixture.

Heat the olive oil in a large ovenproof skillet (preferably cast iron). Add the meatballs and brown them on all sides, about 3 minutes. Place the skillet in the oven to finish cooking the meatballs, 5-7 minutes.

Toss the meatballs with the sauce, garnish with parsley and Parmesan, and serve.

TRIONE VINEYARDS & WINERY

It's fall, so light a fire, sip some wine and stay cozy at home. The days are shorter, the rains are coming, and you want something easy to cook. This stick-to-your-ribs brisket is just the dinner you need.

19550 Geyserville Avenue | Geyserville, CA 95441
707-814-8100
trionewinery.com

BACON-BRAISED BEEF BRISKET

Pair with Trione Alexander Valley Primitivo

SERVES 4

1 tablespoon olive oil

2 pounds beef brisket
(2 1-pound strips)

kosher salt, to taste

fresh ground black pepper,
to taste

4 slices applewood-smoked
bacon, thick cut

1 yellow onion, peeled, large dice

2 carrots, peeled, large dice

3 celery ribs, large dice

6 cloves garlic, smashed

10 crimini mushrooms,
destemmed and halved

1-½ pounds Yukon Gold
potatoes, peeled, large dice

½ bunch fresh thyme

3 cinnamon sticks

2 bay leaf

1 cup Primitivo

1 cup beef stock

In a heavy-bottom sauté pan, heat the olive oil. Season the brisket generously with salt and pepper, and brown it on all sides in the hot oil.

Dice 2 slices of the smoked bacon and brown them in the pan after the brisket is browned. Wrap the remaining 2 slices of bacon around the brisket.

Place all the ingredients in a slow cooker, with the brisket on top. Season the vegetables with salt and pepper. Cook the brisket for 5 hours on the high setting, and serve.

WILLIAMSON WINES

Several of our tasting room staff prepared and served this recipe in March 2013 at a dinner party for 10 guests. The consensus opinion of the group was "awesome recipe." The Rosé of Pinot Noir and a Sauvignon Blanc were served, and nine out of the 10 people voted the rosé as the better pairing with the paella.

134 Matheson Street | Healdsburg, CA 95448
707-433-1500
williamsonwines.com

AUSSIE PAELLA
WITH HERBIE'S SPICES

Pair with Williamson Rosé of Pinot Noir

SERVES 6-8

4 cups chicken stock, hot

2 teaspoons Herbie's Paella Spice Blend

⅓ cup olive oil

2 small chicken breast fillets

2-3 cloves garlic, crushed

1 red bell pepper, seeded and sliced

1-½ cups long-grain rice

12 anchovy fillets

2 tomatoes, peeled and chopped

1 cup shelled peas

8 baby octopus, cleaned and halved

12 green prawns, peeled and tails intact

6 mussels, scrubbed

Add the Herbie's paella mix to the hot stock and set it aside.

Heat the oil in a sauté pan and brown the chicken on both sides. Remove the chicken from the pan and cut each breast into 4 pieces. Add the garlic and red bell pepper to the pan and sauté them until they're soft.

Add the rice and stir to coat the grains. Add the stock with the paella mix and stir through. Arrange the chicken pieces, anchovies, tomatoes and peas on top of the rice mixture.

With the pan lightly covered, cook the paella 20-25 minutes, adding the octopus, prawns and mussels in the last few minutes of cooking. Serve the dish when nearly all of the stock has been absorbed and the mussels have opened. Discard any mussels that do not open.

WILSON WINERY

Pork and apples are a dynamic duo, one of the world's classic flavor combinations. Add smoky bacon, sweet caramelized onions, the tang of apple cider vinegar, and a splash of flavor-boosting Jepson brandy, and the complexity and deliciousness of this dish simply soars.

1960 Dry Creek Road | Healdsburg, CA 95448
707-433-4355
wilsonwinery.com